Inclusive Growth

Dr. N.A. Mujumdar is former Principal Adviser, Reserve Bank of India. At present, he is the Editor of the Indian Journal of Agricultural Economics and also Honorary Professor at the Society for Development Studies.

Dr. Mujumdar began his career as Lecturer in what was then known as the School of Economics, University of Bombay. He was Nuffield Fellow of Oxford University, Oxford, in 1959, and after his return to India, joined the Reserve Bank of India.

The author has also worked, under the auspices of the International Monetary Fund, as Adviser to the Central Banks of five countries: Zambia, Mauritius, Tanzania, Belize and Cambodia. He was Consultant to FAO, ESCAP and the World Bank. He was member of various Working Groups appointed by the Reserve Bank of India and the Planning Commission.

He has published ten books and a number of research papers in various technical journals. Among his recent books are: *Economic Reforms Sans Development* (2004) and *Indian Agriculture in the New Millennium* (a set of 2 volumes co-edited with Uma Kapila, 2006), both published by Academic Foundation, New Delhi.

Inclusive Growth

Development Perspectives in Indian Economy

N A MUJUMDAR

ACADEMIC FOUNDATION
NEW DELHI

www.academicfoundation.com

First published in 2007
by

ACADEMIC FOUNDATION
4772-73 / 23 Bharat Ram Road, (23 Ansari Road),
Darya Ganj, New Delhi - 110 002 (India).
Phones : 23245001 / 02 / 03 / 04.
Fax : +91-11-23245005.
E-mail : academic@vsnl.com
www. academicfoundation.com

Cataloging in Publication Data--DK
Courtesy: D.K. Agencies (P) Ltd. docinfo@dkagencies.com

Mujumdar, N.A., 1930-
Inclusive growth : development perspectives in Indian economy / N.A. Mujumdar
p. cm.
Includes index.
ISBN 13: **9788171886296**
ISBN 10: 8171886299

1. India--Economic policy--1991- 2. Monetary policy --India. 3. Agriculture--Economic aspects--India. 4. Rural credit--India. 5. Banks and banking--India. I. Title.

DDC 338.954 22

Typeset by Italics India, New Delhi.
Printed and bound in India.

10 9 8 7 6 5 4 3 2 1

To my grandson

Jayant

Contents

Part III

Banking and Finance

Part IV

Development Perspectives

Introduction

It appears that idioms and metaphors of development economics keep on changing from time to time. Suddenly, the phrase 'Inclusive Growth' has become fashionable as is reflected in the title of the Draft Approach Paper to the Eleventh Five Year Plan—Towards Faster and More Inclusive Growth. This is perhaps a new label to the rather old fashioned concept of 'broad-based and decentralised growth' which some of us have been advocating for many years. The bunch of 19 papers brought together in this book bear testimony to such advocacy.

At the outset, inclusive growth needs to be contextualised. Even if the 8 per cent GDP growth targeted in the Eleventh Plan is sustained, and export growth is maintained at say 15 to 20 per cent, the organised sectors like large and medium industries, IT sector, etc. can do precious little to tackle the problems of unemployment, poverty, and hunger. In other words, employment generated autonomously by the normal process of growth will fall far short of the requirements. The policy thrust will have to be, per force, on broad-based decentralised growth, if the macroeconomic objectives of reducing unemployment and poverty are to be achieved. Viewed from this perspective, inclusive growth has become a growth and development imperative: growth because a high GDP growth like the 8 per cent targeted in the Eleventh Plan (2007-2012) can be sustained only if other sectors or segments of the economy, which have been sluggish because of a number of reasons including policy neglect, can be activated. Development, because this is perhaps the best route by which the bulk of the poor can be provided with livelihood and food security.

In a way 'the inclusiveness' may be said to have two dimensions: one, in terms of sectors or segments of the economy which need to be brought into the fold of a vibrant economy; and two, in terms of enabling sections of the population, whom the growth process has bypassed, to fully engage themselves with the development process.

This approach is a welcome correction to the 'growth-only' policies of the last 15 years since the inception of economic reforms in 1991. This phase when the policy focus was on liberalisation, market-led growth, fiscal correction, promotion of private and foreign investment, development of the capital market and creation of an environment of consumerism, can be categorised as an 'era of exclusion'. As the papers in the book demonstrate concretely, during this phase, a large number of small farmers were pushed out of commercial banks' loan-portfolio. Furthermore, a large number of poor families were thrown out of the public distribution system because of the new definition of below the poverty line (BPL) families. Due to the continuous raising of the issue prices of foodgrains, the concessionally priced foodgrains became increasingly inaccessible to the poor. Ironically enough, India, which is the abode of the largest number of chronically underfed and undernourished people in the world, exported a huge quantity of 27 million tonnes of foodgrains during the three consecutive years 2001-02 to 2003-04. Inspired by market theology, Indian policymakers appear to have become cortically blind during this phase in the sense that their eyes could see but their brains could not register the image of what they saw. Alas! little did our policymakers realise that that brand of development economics, founded on market theology, which only exhorts us to raise the production of foodgrains, without ever bothering to find out the *modus operandi* by which foodgrains so produced could reach the bulk of the needy, is of little relevance to the contemporary Indian situation.

It is perhaps the search for an alternative paradigm of growth which has now led the policymakers to 'inclusive growth', which is pro-poor and which may provide an answer to the dilemma faced by the market-led development approach.

In this context, the contemporary experience of China is illuminating. China, whose macroeconomic parameters were comparable to those of India provides the most fascinating example of such inclusive growth. Today, China's manufacturing power is reshaping the world economy. The world capital labour ratio has nearly halved because of the incorporation of its new labour force in the global economy. Analytically, what is important to highlight is that this impressive growth in manufacturing and even the double-digit GDP growth sustained over more than two decades would not have been able, by themselves, to make a significant dent on the levels of unemployment or of poverty. It was the vibrant rural non-farm sector which played a critical role in the success story of drastically reducing poverty and unemployment. China's Township and Village Enterprises (TVEs) provided increasing job opportunities outside agriculture, thereby augmenting sources of household income. The phenomenal growth of this sector is demonstrated by the fact that its contribution to GDP rose to nearly one-third of total GDP in 2004, from practically zero in 1952.

All those involved in the development of the Indian economy—banks, cooperatives, development finance institutions, NGOs, and administrators—will have to rethink their own strategies in response to the new emphasis being given on 'inclusive growth'. Perhaps the first step in this direction is to identify the segments of the rural economy, on the analogy of the Chinese experience referred to above, which have so far not attracted adequate attention of policymakers but which deserve to be focused on in the new strategy.

The papers included in this book have sought to identify the following, as illustrative of the segments on which policy should focus. Foremost among the sluggish sectors is agriculture which is central to India's economic development. It recorded in the first three years of the Tenth Plan an annual average growth of less than 2 per cent as against the target of 4 per cent stipulated. Even after the potential of large and medium irrigation projects is fully exploited, about 60 per cent of cultivable land would continue to be under the dry farming system. Hence future agricultural growth will have to be necessarily water-centric. This is particularly so, because the more fertile lands like in the Punjab-Haryana region perhaps have reached a growth plateau. Five interconnected programmes assume significance in this context: watershed development programme, both macro and micro, rainwater harvesting and conservation, renovation of traditional water bodies, improving water use efficiency in the public irrigation works, notably in canals, and promotion of micro irrigation technology, like drip and sprinkler irrigation systems. The bunch of other projects is heterogenous: animal husbandry, horticulture, fisheries, development of waste lands and forests, soil conservation, drainage and flood control, organic farming with organic seed and compost preparatory, food processing, storage, warehousing and marketing.

The moot point is that the loan-portfolios of banks and other rural lending institutions must begin to reflect the more diversified credit support to these emerging segments and not merely support crop production, important though the latter will continue to be. The illustrative segments we have chosen to discuss would offer projects which would be viable and hence perfectly bankable. This is particularly true of water-centric development of agriculture.

The financial system, especially banks, face a formidable task in addressing this issue. Obviously, commercial banks cannot easily access these scattered and widely dispersed segments of the economy. This raises the issue of the new architecture of the rural credit delivery system. The instrumentality of micro-credit institutions to access these segments has proved successful. The experiment of micro finance through the conduit of self-help groups (SHGs) has shown that transaction costs of banks could be reduced drastically and repayment rates can be as high as 90 per cent. Commercial banks, cooperatives and even Regional Rural Banks (RRBs) must move towards spreading this model and spreading it fast. Yet another model of linking non-government organisations (NGOs) and SHGs with banks has emerged with Reserve Bank of India (RBI) recently advising banks to use the services of NGOs, SHGs, micro finance institutions (MFIs) and civil society organisations (CSOs) as intermediaries in providing financial and banking services. One hopes that some sort of linkage between banks and the ground level organisations would emerge soon and that rural credit would flow to these segments in adequate quantum and at reasonable interest rates. RBI will have to play a proactive role in terms of evolving area-specific baskets of projects which can be financed by banks. RBI should also explore the desirability of putting in place credit guarantee schemes or interest rate subsidies to specific micro-credit institutions. Inclusive growth in the real sector depends, to a considerable extent on the efficacy with which the rural credit delivery system extends its support to this process.

It is obvious that inclusive growth is a far more complicated process, involving micro planning, evolving area specific solutions and participation of a number of actors—panchayati raj institutions, State and Central Governments, and NGOs, SHGs, etc. It may be useful to attempt to blend the projects under inclusive umbrella with the existing schemes like the Rural Employment Guarantee Schemes or the Food-for-Work programmes. Inclusive growth also demands a committed bureaucracy and more imaginative policymakers, from both of whom a proactive role is warranted.

In this Introduction, I have sought to merely synthesise the outcomes of detailed discussions in the papers included in the book with a view to giving a flavour of the main theme underlying the book. For an in-depth discussion of any specific aspects the reader is invited to refer to the relevant papers.

It may sound rather ironical but if inclusive growth has gained prominence recently, it is because development perspective is embedded in it.

Once again, my grateful thanks to Dr. Uma Kapila who has always taken a personal interest in my books and ensured their timely publication. I am indeed beholden to her.

— N.A. Mujumdar

Part I

Risk Philosophy and Rural Credit

1

Risks, Uncertainties and Rural Credit in Indian Agriculture

I

INTRODUCTION

Historically, Indian agriculture has been subject to various types of risks and uncertainties, the most prominent of which is drought. It is not surprising that the first generation textbooks on the Indian economy described, graphically, Indian agriculture as a gamble in monsoons. Although, we have today moved quite a distance away from the situation of yesteryears, with the net irrigated area forming nearly 40 per cent of the net sown area, the basic threat of failure of monsoons continues to haunt the Indian economy. The most recent drought of 2002-03, when agricultural production declined by 7 per cent demonstrates this point. Apart from drought, there are other sources of risk in agriculture like devastating cyclones, floods, plant diseases or pests or even a sudden drying up of tubewells. In addition to production risks, there is the price risk faced by the farmer: either the prices of farm inputs may rise suddenly, or prices of farm output—or products—may decline sharply, or both. These and other risks in agriculture which we would discuss later, affect adversely profitability of farming business and hence, has important implications also for bankers or lenders to farmers in general. Analytically it is useful to discuss, separately, risks faced by individual farmer on the one hand and risks in lending to agriculture as perceived by bankers on the other. Although, these are two sides of the same coin, as it were, it is useful to discuss the two facets separately, since we seek to analyse the role of credit in tackling risks in agriculture. There is yet another dimension to the whole issue: the perception of bankers of risks in agriculture may not be necessarily and always rational, as we shall analyse subsequently. Nonetheless, such perceptions do impact both the availability and the cost of credit to the farmer. Both these are perceptions at the micro level: the farmer looking at his individual farm business and the banker looking at the individual farmer as a potential borrower.

The difficulty with the Indian monetary and credit policymakers of the 1990s, when financial sector reforms were introduced as part of the process of liberalisation and globalisation of the Indian economy, was that they sought to mimic the concepts and models of risk in the developed countries like the USA or Australia. Hence, the story of risks in agriculture ended here. Mechanistic transplantation of models from the developed economies on to the Indian soil has led to disastrous results, for agricultural growth, as we will spell out later.

In a developing economy, it is necessary to adopt a holistic approach to the assessment of risks in agriculture; only such an approach can pave the way for a meaningful assessment of risks and for finding practical solutions to minimise the incidence of these risks. It is here that we move into the realm of what can be broadly described as risk philosophy. The measures taken by the monetary and credit policymakers in the 1990s were not, alas, grounded in such a risk philosophy appropriate to the Indian socio-economic milieu. Basically, there is a need to superimpose, on the two micro perceptions of risks mentioned earlier, a macro perception of policymakers, whose objective should be to reduce the incidence of risks in the agricultural sector taken as a whole; and furthermore, use credit, *inter alia,* as an instrument to achieve this overall objective. In other words, the risk models we have imported from developed countries, including the Basel models, take risks as given at any point of time and then seek to cover such risks. In contrast, in a developing economy like that of India it should be the medium-term objective of monetary and credit policies to seek to change the risk profile of the agricultural sector itself; and credit policy should become an important ingredient of the macroeconomic management package designed to eventually change the risk profile of agriculture. Credit, both short-term and long-term, should be viewed, in this context, as both a growth-enhancing and risk-reducing instrument. Credit to support investment in irrigations of any type is a case in point. This sums up the risk philosophy appropriate to the Indian situation.

In the banking sector reforms of the 1990s such macro perception of risk was conspicuous by its absence. The whole approach to assessment of risks in the agricultural sector and consequently to shaping agricultural lending policy was faulted because the monetary and credit policymakers of the 1990s were soaked in the market theology of the International Monetary Fund (IMF) and World Bank. Directed lending is bad and hence should be abhorred. All subsidies including interest rate subsidies, militate against market forces and hence abolish interest rate subsidies to agriculture. Financial sector reforms, taken as a whole, created an adversarial environment for rural credit, giving a misconceived impression, that lending to agriculture or priority sectors in general is a high-risk business. No wonder bankers, particularly public sector bankers, shied away from lending to agriculture, thus converting the 1990s into a lost decade for agriculture.

I have analysed in *extensio* the adverse impact of financial sector reforms on rural credit elsewhere providing statistical and other evidence in support of this main theme.[1] Here, I will be content with merely utilising the conclusions of the analysis.

'Monetary authority's approach to banking reforms clearly reflect an amateurish appreciation of the relevance of these reforms to development. We need to look at the following four areas of reform: Basel Norms, Statutory Liquidity Ratio requirements, Non-performing Assets (NPAs) and Subsidies.

First, during this phase of reforms implementing the Basel norms became almost the sole preoccupation of RBI. The policymakers appeared to emphasise that ensuring capital adequacy, and provisioning norms are all what the banking reforms about. The hurry with which RBI sets out to implement these two norms gives the impression that making the Indian banking system Basel-compliant was regarded as the *summum bonum* of banking reforms. In the process, the ground realities of the Indian rural sector were drowned by rhetorics of reforms. RBI had neither the time nor the inclination to look at the rural credit delivery system, the health of which was allowed to deteriorate. Supply-led rural credit expansion, promotional initiatives, proper appraisal, monitoring and follow-up of rural loan projects—all these ingredients of innovative rural credit policy pursued since the latter part of 1950s, following the recommendations of the Report of the All India Rural Credit Survey, 1954, were given the go by.

---

1. Mujumdar, N.A. (2002). *Financial Sector Reforms and India's Economic Development*, Volume 1 and 2. Academic Foundation, New Delhi. Particularly see the Section: "Financial Sector Reforms (Vol. 1) and Rural Credit (Vol. 2)".

Second, risk perceptions of bankers is, again, a relative concept. Inspired by market theology, RBI suddenly discovered that Government of India should begin to raise resources from the banking sector at market related interest rates, with the result that yields on Government securities soared, at one point, to 14 per cent. Such an attractive yield on a zero-transaction cost and zero-risk instrument like the Government security tempted public sector bankers to invest massively in Government securities well beyond the Statutory Liquidity Ratio (SLR) requirement. It may be recalled that following the recommendation of the Narasimham Committee on Financial Sector Reforms (1991), the SLR was reduced to 25 per cent of Net Demand and Time Liabilities (NDTL). Ironically, the investment-deposit ratio of the banking system recorded a quantum jump from a required ratio of 25 per cent of NDTL to 38 per cent or even 40 per cent during the 1990s. In other words, investment in Government securities crowded out priority sectors including the agricultural sector, from the banking systems resources.[2]

How can one expect bankers to lend to a small farmer at say 12 per cent or at even lower rate when one can realise a 14 per cent return by investing in a zero-risk instrument? The phenomenon of excess holding of Government securities continues to plague the utilisation of banking sector resources of public sector banks (PSBs) even today, with the investment-deposit ratio touching 44 per cent in September 2004. In absolute terms, such excess holdings had reached a staggering figure of Rs. 2,67,328 crore at end-March 2004.[3] In other words, by providing such an attractive avenue for deployment of banking sector resources, through flawed interest rate policy, funds which would otherwise have supported productive sectors like agriculture were siphoned off to support Government consumption.

Both these reforms had the net effect of making a dent on the resources potentially available for deployment to priority sectors including agriculture. Basel norms required earmarking of resources for capital adequacy and provisioning. Of course, excess investment in Government Securities was technically voluntary but prompted by explicit interest rate policy. Also, in the bankers' mind, priority sectors were relegated to the second order priority.

---

2. See the Section on Public Debt Management in the book cited in footnote 1.
3. Reddy, Y.V. (2004). *Mid-Term Review of Monetary and Credit Policy for the Year 2004-05*, Reserve Bank of India, October 26, p. 11.

Third, Non-performing Assets (NPAs). Provisioning norms made the bankers suddenly risk conscious; and priority sectors accounted for 50 per cent of the total NPAs of public sector banks in 1995. No wonder priority sectors came to be regarded as "untouchable" by PSBs. How far NPAs could be treated as a true reflection of intrinsic risks in the concerned sector? We will examine this issue in-depth later. At this stage the only other point that needs to be underlined is that there are factors other than intrinsic risks which shape NPAs. For instance, the historical baggage inherited by the rural credit system should not be conveniently forgotten. The reference here is to the erosion of repayment ethics by the 'loan melas' of yesteryears and the 'write-offs' of rural loans by some populist State Governments. Policymakers of the 1990s lacked this historical perspective. Ultimately, it is such episodes in financial history which shape the NPAs of banks and cooperative credit institutions. We will see later how banks have been able, subsequently, to reduce drastically incremental NPAs in the priority sectors by proper appraisal and effective monitoring of rural lending. Governance is also an important element which shapes NPAs.

Finally, subsidies. Indian policymakers of the 1990s whose expertise in development economics stemmed from the IMF/World Bank theology seem to conveniently overlook the basic fact that agriculture in developed countries like the USA and Organisation for Economic Co-operation Development (OECD) countries is highly subsidised in a variety of ways, both domestic and export subsidies. For instance, global agricultural subsidies are estimated to add up some $ 360 billion annually or nearly a billion dollars a day. Of the total, 80 per cent is accounted for by OECD countries.[4] These subsidies continue to persist even in the current World Trade Organisaion (WTO) regime.

In many of these developed countries, financial subsidies are also extended to facilitate flow of cheaper credit to agriculture and small enterprises.[5] More concretely, take the case of US farm credit interest rates. In July-September 2004, the rates were as follows: interest on new farm loans averaged 7.22 per cent for operating loans, 7.28 per cent for machinery and intermediate term loans, and 6.82 per cent for real estate loans.[6] Compare these lending rates with the 12 per cent interest charged

---

4. Anderson, Pinstrup (2002). *Indian Agriculture in a Globalising World*, Exim Bank, Mumbai.
5. NABARD (2004). See: Box: "Can Lower Rates of Interest be an Objective of Reforms?", in *Pricing of Crop Loans by Cooperative Banks*.
6. *The Main Street Economist*, Federal Reserve Bank of Kansas City, February 2004.

by banks in India till recently to small farmers. When major exporters cry hoarse that interest rates on export credit in India should be comparable to those in say the USA, both the Government and RBI are eager to comply with the request. Of course, the IMF/World Bank theology supports this plea. Our farm lobby may not be exactly mute but it has not adequately captured the nuances of interest rate policy. The central point is that we need not be apologetic about subsidising agriculture and credit to agriculture, notwithstanding IMF/World Bank theology.

It is, thus, clear that risks or perceptions of risks in agriculture are shaped by a constellation of factors, all of which can be captured by an appropriate risk philosophy. There is no unique textbook formula for measuring risks in agriculture and hence, any attempt to build a risk premium into lending rates of agriculture, as we seem to have been doing in the 1990s, is a misconceived exercise, empty of economic meaning.

Risks in agriculture need to be tackled in a more holistic and strategic manner than what is sought to be done by merely mimicking mechanistically banking models of the USA or Australia. In the Indian context, taking a macro view of risk, credit should play a dual role of growth-enhancement and risk-reduction. Changing the risk profile of agriculture itself, thus becomes an explicit objective of credit policy. Risk philosophy which provides the broad matrix within which rural credit policy needs to be shaped should be firmly anchored in development imperatives, which will be spelt out later.

Ensuring a critical minimum of 4 per cent agricultural growth in the coming years can alone sustain a 7 or 8 per cent GDP growth in the medium-term as envisaged by the Tenth Five Year Plan. It is the business of rural credit policy to facilitate and sustain the required rate of agricultural growth. Secondly, the risk reducing role of credit should be factored into the rural credit policy, including interest rate policy. This provides the rationale for concessional lending to certain avenues of agricultural development. It is thus, clear that attempts to build a risk premium into the lending rates to agriculture in the 1990s were flawed both in theory and practice: in theory, because the borrowed concept of risk does not even seek to capture the special circumstances of developing countries much less the India-specific situation. In practice, because the blind application of this concept to policy measures may prove to be counter-productive. Thirdly, the term 'agriculture' has to be construed in an extended sense, which would, of course, include allied sectors like livestock, fisheries and forestry. Raising rural income levels would involve not only higher agricultural growth but also raising the production levels of products like milk, meat, fish, poultry, vegetables and fruits. Besides promoting diversification of agriculture, there is a need for value addition for increasing rural employment and incomes. Post-harvest activities such as storage, transportation, processing and marketing become important in this context.[7]

In addition, investment avenues which would go some way towards raising the production capabilities of agriculture should also be covered suitably. Looked at from this holistic viewpoint, risk philosophy lends a new perspective to rural lending policy as also to risk management by banks and other lending institutions.

The present guidelines issued by RBI to banks for risk management would perhaps need to be reframed with respect to agriculture and allied sectors in the light of these considerations. Fortunately, more recent policy initiatives, of the United Progressive Alliance (UPA) Government in the area of rural credit as reflected in the National Common Minimum Programme (NCMP), indicate clearly that wisdom is at last beginning to draw on the contemporary Indian policymakers.

II

CHANGING RISK PERCEPTIONS OF BANKERS

It may be useful to begin the discussion on risks in agriculture and the role of credit with the changes in risk perceptions of bankers; because ultimately, it is these perceptions of bankers which shape the mindsets and attitudes of bankers to agriculture. The risk perceptions of bankers, particularly public sector bankers seem to have undergone a perceptible change in the 1990s, when the financial sector reforms were introduced as a part of the process of liberalisation and globalisation of the Indian economy. Historically, the risk perceptions have gone through three distinct phases: first, the post-nationalisation of bank phase extending from 1969 to 1990; second, during the phase of banking sector reforms say from 1990 to 2004; and third, the period subsequent to 2004 when the NCMP was announced by the UPA Government. This programme envisages doubling of agricultural credit in the next three years. We will later have occasion to examine whether such changes in perception of risk

7. Mohan, Rakesh (2004). "Agricultural Credit in India: Status, Issues and Future Agenda", *Reserve Bank of India Bulletin*, November.

by bankers were rational, in the sense of being technically justifiable. What is equally important is that all these changes were policy-induced in the sense that the changes reflected bankers' response to the policy measures, taken during the relevant period, by the Government and/or by the RBI. In this sense, the changes in risk perceptions of bankers were reactive and not proactive. The point that needs to be driven home is that policy measures can create an environment in which changes in bankers perception could take place irrespective of whether the intrinsic technical ingredients of risks in agriculture have remained unchanged or not.

The phenomenal expansion of banking in India in the post-nationalisation period, both in terms of widening and deepening of the banking system, is unprecedented in the history of World banking. Bringing the rural sector, not only agriculture, into the mainstream of modern banking was a stupendous achievement. In this dramatic transformation, both the Government at the Centre and States, the RBI and PSBs played a crucial role. The techniques employed for extending the reach of banks, the training imparted to the bank personnel involved, and their travails and tribulations—all these have been chronicled by National Institute of Bank Management (NIBM) in an excellent book.[8] There are two important lessons to be derived from this empirical experience, to which the attention of contemporary banking policymakers needs to be drawn. First, the phenomenal expansion of rural credit witnessed during this phase was essentially supply-led and not demand-derived. There is an enormous potential demand for institutional credit in the rural sector but for translating this potential demand for credit into effective demand, the banker or the credit supplying agencies in general have to do some homework: explore and identify such potential demand, and assist in giving a concrete shape to such demand for credit and credit worthy projects. This task of giving a concrete shape to potential demand is as important as the task of fine-tuning the supply-side of credit. The proactive role played by banks during this phase in generating effective demand for credit, is thus, obvious. In sharp contrast, banking sector reforms in the 1990s seemed to have focussed only on the fine-tuning of the supply side while neglecting almost totally the demand side. Secondly, banking officials at that point of time were not being paid princely sums. Those experts who, today, argue that PSBs are not attracting competent officers because their emoluments are nowhere near those of foreign bankers would do well, if they, read the book mentioned above. These

8. Rao, K. Dinker (2002). *Taking, Banking to the People—NIBM's Role*, NIBM, Pune.

pioneering efforts of PSBs, ultimately, enabled agriculture and priority sectors to claim their legitimate share in the commercial banks' resources. Indian agriculture during this period was exposed to far greater risks than what it is today. This did not deter public sector banks from aggressively lending to agriculture. In fact, there is enough documentary evidence to show that the Green Revolution was facilitated, to a considerable extent, by bank credit which enabled a large number of farmers to adopt the new farm technology.

Regarding the second phase, if the rural credit institutions find themselves in a moribund state today, this is largely attributable to the financial sector reforms introduced in the 1990s. In the milieu of the new banking culture fostered by reforms, lending to agriculture or priority sectors generally became unfashionable. The relative magnitude of the flow of credit to agriculture shrank and the interest rate regime which was designed to pamper the private corporate sector openly discriminated against agriculture. Even PSBs merrily defaulted, for many years during the 1990s, on the credit targets of 18 per cent of net bank credit to agriculture and 40 per cent of net bank credit to priority sectors. The RBI, which was obsessed with implementing the Basel norms as the main thrust of banking reforms, winked at the defaults. While the priority sector target has been attained during the last couple of years, the target for agriculture continues to remain unattained: lending to agriculture is around 15 per cent today, as compared to the target of 18 per cent of net bank credit. In the new banking culture, nurtured by reforms, the focus of PSBs was on the three Cs'—namely, Corporate elite, Consumer credit and Capital market related activities. For instance, PSBs had enough resources to extend a bridge loan to enterprises like M.S. Shoes, but they did not have funds to support the production of sugar in Maharashtra. There was an actual disenfranchisement of rural borrowers, the total number of small farmers borrowing from banks declined in absolute terms.[9] For the priority sector as a whole, the number of accounts declined from 349 lakhs in 1991 to 273 lakhs in 2001. This episode reflects the totally changed mindset of public sector bankers during the reform phase.

While this is the status of availability of credit, the story of the cost of credit is equally depressing. While highly rated corporate entities could raise money from banks or PSBs at interest rates as low as 6 or 7 per cent, the small farmer was required to pay a rate of 12 per cent till recently. It was left to the Government of India to reduce the lending rate to small

9. Mujumdar, N.A. (2001). *The New Architecture of the Rural Credit System*, University of Mumbai.

farmers to 9 per cent only in August 2003. The World Bank and IMF continue to peddle their market theology and the RBI's response appeared to be, till recently, those of a suppliant student. A recent World Bank Development Policy Review on India, states: "Rural access to finance is further constrained by the inefficiency of rural financial markets, characterised by interest rate 'caps' requiring banks to price small loans within a range of 2 per cent above or below the prime lending rate. These 'caps' have a perverse effect of rationing credit to small rural borrowers, because banks prefer not to lend at these rates. That drives small rural borrowers to borrow from the informal sector, where money lenders charge exorbitant rates: Hence the World Bank recommends: "Liberalising interest rates by removing the existing interest rate 'caps' for small loans".[10]

RBI seems to be only too willing to join the chorus, "Secondly, there is the issue of stepping up loans to relatively disadvantaged sections of borrowers including small and medium enterprises and the agricultural sector. To many of the borrowers in these sectors it is, in fact, the availability of credit more than the price of credit which is of prime importance. This is especially so because interest rates in informal markets which serve as an alternative to bank finance, particularly in rural areas, are sometimes at usurious levels relative to the formal sector."[11] One can forgive the World Bank for being innocent of recent financial history of India but what about the RBI.

RBI's neglect of agriculture and the rural sector generally was total during the 1990s: it failed to arrest the deterioration of the health of all the institutions involved in rural credit: PSBs, Cooperative credit institutions and RRBs—all of which showed high NPAs. In other words, the financial sector reforms which were transplanted from the so-called Basel norms were ill-conceived and unrelated to the specific socio-economic milieu of the Indian soil, and they succeeded in creating an adversarial environment for rural credit. In fact the credit-deposit ratio of RRBs declined sharply over the 1990s, indicating a reverse flow of funds from the rural to the urban areas. Even RRBs were permitted to invest in the Public Sector Unit (PSU) bonds. No wonder, the annual average rate of agricultural growth decelerated sharply from 4.7 per cent in the Eighth Five Year Plan to only 2 per cent in the Ninth Plan.[12]

---

10. World Bank (2003). *India: Sustaining Reform, Reducing Poverty*, Oxford University Press, New Delhi, p. 84.
11. Reserve Bank of India (2004). *Annual Report*, Mumbai, pp. 122-123.
12. *op. cit.* footnote 9.

It is indeed gratifying to note that the Tenth Five Year Plan endorses my viewpoint: "It is being evident, however, that the organised financial sector in India is either unable or unwilling to finance a range of activities that are of crucial importance both for growth and development. Agriculture, unorganised manufacturing and services, and various types of infrastructure are instances of such sectors. The recent financial sector reforms have naturally focused primarily on improving the viability and stability of financial institutions without adequately addressing this issue. It is therefore necessary to consider methods of encouraging the financial sector to finance such activities, without impinging on its viability or compromising on prudential concerns."[13] One thing should be made quite clear: it was not 'inability' of banks because the banking system was highly liquid during the 1990s, with the credit-deposit ratio hovering around 50 per cent.

How is it that PSBs discovered suddenly in the 1990s, that agriculture was a 'high risk' business, potentially capable of generating high NPAs? This is how charging a high risk premium to agriculture was sought to be justified. In terms of risk ingredient characterising agriculture, there was perhaps no change. If anything Indian agriculture was relatively less exposed to risks in the 1990s than what it was in 1970s. How then one could justify the treatment meted out to agriculture in the 1990s by PSBs?

One can seek the analogy from India's political history. There was a class which later came to be known as 'Macalay's Bastards', a group of elite, legally and constitutionally trained, upper-middle class Indian men. The freedom movement was initially confined to this select group.[14] It was Mahatma Gandhi who transformed subsequently this freedom struggle into a mass movement involving farmers and the common man. On the same analogy, we may categorise the three Cs' mentioned earlier, as 'Basel's Bastards'. The banking sector reforms and economic reforms in general, seem to have been aimed at pampering the private corporate elite and at providing artificial props to develop the capital market, goading PSBs to involve themselves increasingly, both directly and indirectly, in the capital market and related activities, facilitating external commercial borrowings, and ushering in a low interest rate regime for corporate sector.

---

13. Planning Commission, *Tenth Five Year Plan*, New Delhi, Vol.II, p. 273.
14. Bilgrami, Akeel (2003). "Gandhi, The Philosopher", *Economic and Political Weekly*, September 27.

In a way, this perversion of priorities of development in terms of focusing on the 'Basel's Bastards', crowded out agriculture and priority sectors generally from the banking sector's resources. The ostensible reason for this reordering of priorities by bankers was that in terms of risk assessment for provisioning requirements under the Basel regime, as we will discuss later, agriculture came to be regarded as a 'high risk' business. And hence, building a risk premia into lending rate resulted in a relatively higher lending rate for agriculture. Instead of discriminating in favour of agriculture, as in the case of even developed countries, the financial system began to discriminate against agriculture. Superseding these developments was the emergence of Government securities, as the high-yielding avenue of investment, with zero-risk and zero-transaction cost. As we have seen earlier, public sector bankers were happy to 'flood' the Government securities market with their 'surplus' resources after meeting the demands of the three Cs'. This was the new banking culture nurtured by the banking reforms of the 1990s, which stands in sharp contrast to the culture of the 1970s. We now need, in a manner of speaking, a Mahatma Gandhi in the financial sector to correct these distorted priorities and to redirect financial flows, both investment and working capital, towards reviving agriculture and towards financing a whole range of activities designed to promote decentralised development.

The banking community seems to have suddenly become rather insensitive to credit needs of the rural sector. Take, for example, the document, 'Banking Industry Vision 2010' produced by the Indian Bank's Association (IBA) in 2003.[15] This 55-page document devotes only 3 paragraphs to rural credit (pages 42 and 43). It is unfortunate that this document does not even take cognisance of the problems of rural branches of banks, their inability to meet the target for agricultural credit despite the persisting low credit-deposit ratios. For the IBA, God is in heaven and everything is alright with rural credit. If the document demonstrates anything, it is IBA's ability to mouth empty rhetoric's about market theology, "the banking system is expected to reorient its approach to rural lending. 'Going Rural' could be the new market mantra. Rural market comprises 74 per cent of the population, 41 per cent of middle class and 58 per cent of disposable income... Banks' approach to the rural lending will be guided mainly by commercial considerations in future." This almost reads like a script by Hindustan Lever executives exploring rural

15. Indian Banks Association (2003). *Banking Industry Vision 2010*, November, Mumbai.

markets for their products! In the final phase, happily, the same PSBs which shunned lending to agriculture, have begun to sing a different note after the UPA announced in 2004, its target of doubling agricultural credit in the next three years. Now the same bankers are highlighting the excellent repayment performance in the areas of priority sector lending: the repayment is more than 90 per cent in the case of Punjab National Bank. Suddenly, there is a flurry of activity, with many Chairmen of PSBs and Senior Executives being actually on the rural circuit promoting rural credit.[16] One begins to wonder whether these are the same bankers bitten by the Basel norms who shunned lending to the rural sector on the specious plea that such lending would breed higher NPAs. In any case, the new dispensation warrants a total change in the attitudes of public sector banks to rural lending.

III

CAPITAL ADEQUACY AND PROVISIONING NORMS, AND PRIORITY SECTORS

The obsession of policy makers of the 1990s with mechanistic implementation of Basel norms, particularly capital adequacy and provisioning norms, without taking into account India-specific development imperatives has led to a false perception of PSBs about risks in agriculture and lending to agriculture. Credit market is different from commodity markets where supply of and demand for a commodity determines the price. Credit is a commando instrument, the distribution of which across sectors determines the trajectories of growth and development. In the process of implementation of these norms with a messianic zeal, sound or sensible banking fell prey to overemphasis on forms of banking, at the cost of substance of banking. Implementation of these norms became a sort of fad, perhaps treating this as a quick-fix tool for coping with emerging risks in bank lending.

Let us look at the rationale that the Reserve Bank of India provides for implementation of these norms. First, about Capital Adequacy: "1.1 With a view to adopting to Basel Committee framework on capital adequacy norms which takes into account the elements of risk in various types of assets in the balance sheet as well as off-balance sheet business and also

16. "Bank of Target: Head Honchos Hit Rural Trail", *Economic Times*, September 9, 2004.

strengthen the capital base of banks, Reserve Bank of India decided in April 1992 to introduce a risk assets ratio system for banks (including foreign banks) in India, as a capital adequacy measure".[17]

"1.2 Essentially, under the above system the balance sheet assets, non-funded items and other off-balance sheet exposures are assigned weights according to the prescribed risks weights and banks have to maintain unimpaired capital funds equivalent to the prescribed ratio on the aggregate of the risks weighted assets and other exposures on an ongoing basis."[18]

Banks were required to maintain a minimum Capital to Risk-weighted Assets Ratio (CRAR) norm of 8 per cent on an ongoing basis upto the year ending 31 March, 1999. With effect from the year ending 31 March 2000, banks are required to maintain a minimum CRAR of 9 per cent on an ongoing basis.

Second, about prudential norms: "1.1 In line with the international practices and as per the recommendations made by the pricing may not always work. A bank may have "idle capacity and capital that has not been deployed. While such an institution clearly would not want to make a loan at a negative spread, it would probably view even a small positive spread as worthwhile as long as the added risk was acceptable."[19]

The net impact of these reform measures on priority sectors was two-fold. First, the size of lendable resources of banks shrank to the extent of funds earmarked for meeting capital adequacy and provisioning requirements. Secondly, the squeeze had to be applied to sectors perceived as of high risk: and as mentioned earlier, priority sectors accounted for 50 per cent of NPAs of PSBs in 1995. And further, a risk premium had to be loaded on to the lending rates of such high-risk sectors. Squeeze on credit to agriculture and relatively high lending rate were sought to be justified on the basis of these misconceived concepts. And the rest is history.

---

17. Reserve Bank of India (2002). *Guidance Note on Credit Risk Management*, Mumbai, October 2.
18. Reserve Bank of India (2001). *Prudential Norms on Capital Adequacy: Master Circular*, July 19.
19. Reserve Bank of India (2004). *Prudential Norms on Income Recognition, Assets Classification and Provisioning Pertaining to Advances: Master Circular*, July 17.

IV

RISK MANAGEMENT BY BANKS AND AGRICULTURE

RBI seems to believe that implementing Basel norms is what modernisation of the banking system is all about. Since early 1999, it has been goading banks to introduce effective credit risk management systems. This is clear from the number of guidelines it has issued to banks on this and related subjects.

RBI defines credit risk as, "the possibility of losses associated with dimunition in the credit quality of borrowers or counter parties. In a bank's portfolio, losses stem from outright default due to inability or unwillingness of a customer or a counter-party to meet commitments in relation to lending, trading, settlement and other financial transactions. Admittedly, losses result from reduction in portfolio value arising from actual or perceived deterioration in credit quality. Credit risk emanates from a bank's dealing with an individual, corporate, bank, financial institution or a sovereign."[20]

Banks have been asked to set up a Risk Management Committee and also an independent Credit Risk Management Department. The former will be a Board level Sub-committee including CEO and heads of Credit Market, and Operational Risk Management Committees. It will formulate policy and strategy for integrated risk management. The latter will measure, control and manage credit risk on a bank-wide basis.

The risk measurement and quantification at the transaction level is of great importance in Credit Risk Management and this requires some mathematical or statistical tools. A popular model used to evaluate and price credit risk based on market data is the RAROC (Risk Adjusted Return on Capital) model. This model pioneered by what was then known as the Bankers Trust has now been adopted by virtually all major banks in the US and Europe. The underlying idea seems to be that rather than evaluating the actual or contractually promised annual loan, the lending officer balances the expected interest and fee income against the loan's expected risk.

To quote the RBI: "The Reserve Bank favours, a process of gradual convergence with international standards and best practices with suitable country-specific adaptions. This has also been the guiding principle in the

---

20. Reserve Bank of India (2004). *Guidance Note on Credit Risk Management*, February 3.

approach to the New Basel Accord. Having decided in principle, in April 2003, to adopt the Basel Accord, the Reserve Bank is overseeing a road map for migration to Basel II with reviews of progress made at quarterly intervals. To begin with, all banks in India will adopt the standardised Approach for Credit Risk and Basic Indicator Approach for operational risk. After adequate skills are developed, both in banks and at supervisory levels, some banks may be allowed to migrate to the Internal Ratings Based (IRB) Approach."[21]

Wading through the 54 page, highly technical and jargon-ridden document of RBI: 'Risk Management Systems in Banks: Guidelines' issued in 1999, one wonders how many bankers at the operational level could actually follow these guidelines, let alone implement them meaningfully. Enclosed with the Manual are two Bank for International Settlement (BIS) Papers: one on 'Stress testing' and the other on 'Back testing'. Banks, are asked to "develop stress capabilities to undertake tests to capture adverse effects of extreme volatile conditions or outlier events." Although the BIS papers are themselves apologetic about the tentative nature of these tests. RBI seems to be over-enthusiastic to educate PSBs. To get a flavour of the rigours of the risk management system, let us take the stress test.

"Banks that use the internal models approach for meeting market risk capital requirements must have in place a rigorous and comprehensive stress testing programme. Stress testing to identify events or influences that could greatly impact banks is a key component of a bank's assessment of its capital position."

"Banks' stress scenarios need to cover a range of factors that can create extraordinary losses or gains in trading portfolios, or make the control of risk in those portfolios very difficult. These factors include loss-probability events in all major types of risks, including the various components of market, credit and operational risks. Stress scenarios need to shed light on the impact of such events on positions that display both linear and non-linear price characteristics (i.e. options and instruments that have options like characteristics) (Page 46 of the BIS paper: "Amendment to the Capital Accord to Incorporate Market Risks).

Again, take the case of 'Back testing'. The Basel Paper on 'Supervisory Framework for the use of Back testing in conjunction with the Internal Model Approach to Market Risk Capital Requirements' itself is rather apologetic about the tentative nature of the test: "As a technique of

21. Reserve Bank of India. *Annual Report, 2003-04*, p. 122.

evaluating the quality of a firm's risk management model, back testing continues to evolve" (page 1). Nonetheless the paper "urges banks to develop the capability to perform back tests using both hypothetical and actual training outcomes" (page 4). "These back testing programmes typically consist of a period of comparison of the bank's daily value-at-risk measures with the subsequent daily profit or loss (trading outcome)" (page 2).

RBI seems to have taken pleasure in weaving a whole mythology around risk management system, regurgitating the models and material dished out by BIS. Perhaps these efforts of RBI would have been admirable if only risk management were an academic exercise. Unfortunately for the RBI, the management system has to be translated into action plans at the ground level. As Dr. S.S. Tarapore puts it rather sarcastically, "In this context there is an imperative need, for the RBI to prepare a *Child's Guide* to risk management totally free from jargon language."[22]

There is a more basic point in raising these broader issues of risk management by banks in this study. BIS may be the repository of all knowledge about modern banking in developed countries. The complexities of lending to agriculture and related rural sectors cannot be reduced to a grand formula that is hostile to nuances. But surely nobody including RBI could credit BIS with sound knowledge of the intricacies of lending to agriculture in developing countries. It is here that 'suitable country-specific adaptations' become necessary. The risk management system propounded by RBI is certainly not appropriate for agriculture. The misguided measure of charging a relatively high lending rate to agriculture in the 1990s, discussed earlier, is a case in point. Efforts should therefore be made to evolve appropriate guidelines for a risk management system for the agricultural sector. This system should fulfil three conditions. First, the management system should be firmly anchored in an appropriate risk philosophy, the outlines of which have been sketched earlier. Second, the risk-reducing role of credit should be factored into the rural credit policy including interest rate policy. Third, the term 'agriculture' has to be used in an extended sense which would, of course, include allied sectors like livestock, fisheries and forestry. In addition, other investment avenues which would go some way towards raising the production capabilities of agriculture should also be covered. These dimensions of risk management have been spelt out later. It is not too late for the RBI and National Bank

22. Tarapore, S.S. (2004). *Bank Governance and the Role of Non-Executive Directors*, Indian Institute of Management, Bangalore, October 14.

for Agriculture and Rural Development (NABARD) to set up a working group to evolve appropriate guidelines in the light of these considerations. These Guidelines should, among others, identify agriculture and related rural sectors or sub-sectors to which credit support, both short-term and long-term credit, needs to be extended; there should be prioritisation among these sectors and sub-sectors for the purpose of concessional lending; and the preferred mode of lending— whether through NGOs or Panchayati Raj institutions—should also be specified. After all, banking, commercial or cooperative, continues to remain an art.

Nostalgically, one recalls here how the authors of the Report of the All India Rural Credit Survey (1954) sought to adapt admirably the rural lending practices to suit Indian conditions. To overcome the collateral syndrome of banks which was hampering lending to agriculture, they evolved the new concept of crop loans offered on the security of standing crops, irrespective of the ownership of the land concerned. One looks in vain for such innovations in the present Guidelines for Risk Management, particularly with reference to agriculture or priority sectors.

Ironically, Dr. Y.V. Reddy, Governor, RBI has recently made out a case for Public Policy in Risk Management in Agriculture. "Finally ...there is merit in considering a comprehensive public policy on risk management in agriculture, as not only a means of relief for distressed farmers but as an ingredient for more efficient commercialised agriculture."[23] While fully agreeing with this proposal one can only submit that charity must begin at home with a revamped rural credit policy.

V

THE CONCEPTUAL FRAMEWORK OF RISKS AND UNCERTAINTIES IN AGRICULTURE

This quick survey of empirical episodes clearly brought out the fact that the risk perceptions of bankers about agriculture have gone through significant changes during the last three decades. It would be misleading to equate these risk perceptions with intrinsic risk in the sector which could be captured by a statistical formula since the perceptions have been influenced by many factors other than intrinsic risk. In designing policy measures to tackle risks, therefore, one has to be guided by the wider concept of risk philosophy. This brings us to the basic concept of risk. The

23. Reddy, Y.V. (2004). "Rural Credit: Status and Agenda", *Reserve Bank of India Bulletin*, December.

conventional definition of risk is imperfect knowledge where the probabilities of the possible outcomes are known. In contrast, uncertainty exists where such probabilities are not known. In this sense, it is further argued that risk is amenable to statistical measurement, whereas uncertainty is not. In the decision making process in farm management, for instance, this characteristic of 'measurability', is important. However, we have moved away from this conventional distinction since such cases where probabilities are objectively 'known' are an exception rather than the rule.

For the present purpose, we would take the neo-classical definition of risk and uncertainty from the following standard text-book which is currently in popular use: "Coping with Risk in Agriculture."[24]

"We define uncertainty as imperfect knowledge and risk as uncertain consequences, particularly exposure to unfavourable consequences. Risk is therefore not value free, usually indicating an aversion for some of the possible consequences. To illustrate, someone might say that he or she is uncertain about what the weather will be like tomorrow—a value-free statement simply implying imperfect knowledge of the future. But the person might go on to mention that he or she is planning a picnic for the next day and there is a risk that it might rain, indicating lack of indifference as to which of the possible consequences actually eventuates."

Risk is not an exclusive character of agricultural business, because risk is common to all businesses like manufacture or trade. In fact, business profit is sometimes defined as a reward for risk. Our task here, however, is to identify agriculture-specific risks and seek to indicate their implications for the banker or lender in general. Most text-books on risks in agriculture deal with farming business in developed economies and their focus is on spelling out how best the individual farm business can tackle the risks involved, effectively. Thus, it is a micro view of risks, in agriculture, from the point of view of the individual farming unit. Farming business in the developed economies has become far more sophisticated and therefore the methods for the analysis of risky choices have become far more complicated than the more familiar forms of analysis as budgeting method. The various methods which have been evolved for analysing choices involved in risk management are collectively called decision analysis. Furthermore, advances in computer software and

---

24. Hardaker, J.B., R.B.M. Huirne, J.R. Anderson and G. Lien (2004). *Coping with Risk in Agriculture*, CABI Publishing, UK (Second Edition). The discussion pertaining to risk faced by an individual farming unit in a developed economy is drawn from this book.

hardware have made applications of methods of decision analysis simpler and quicker, than in the past for the individual farmers in the more developed economies.

In farming business, it is common to identify four main risks namely, production risk, market risk, institutional risk and personal risk. Collectively, this is called business risk.

i) Production risk stems from the unpredictable nature of the weather and the consequent performance of crops or livestock.

ii) Market risk refers to uncertainties regarding prices of farm input and outputs. Increasingly, farmers the world over, are being exposed to unpredictable markets for inputs and outputs. Thus, price or market risk in the sense of pricing inputs and outputs has become significant over time. Price risk also includes risks arising from fluctuations in exchange rates.

iii) Institutional risk embodies political risk, which means changes in policies or measures which affect agriculture adversely. Changes in price support measures, in input pricing, in marketing arrangements—all these may affect the profitability of farming.

iv) Finally, there are personal risks: prolonged illness of the head of the farming family, or his death is an instance in point.

The totality of these risks is business risk which faces the farming unit—and this is independent of how the unit is financed. Thus, financial risk, is independent of the business risk. There are financial risks in using credit by the farmer. Availability of loan or credit, inadequate quantum of credit, unexpected rise in interest rates on these loans, unexpected calling—in of loan by the lending institution—all these are financial risks faced by the farming unit.

The trouble with our monetary and credit policymakers of the 1990s and also public sector bankers during this period was that their perceptions of risks in agriculture were influenced solely by farming models in developed countries like the US or Australia. Text-books of the type referred to above are entirely based on such models, understandably because they are meant for use in developed economies.

Take the business of a farm as given and assess the risks involved in lending to such a unit. In other words, we interpret the risk in lending, taking the farm as it is situated at a given point of time. This sort of approach may be alright for farming in a developed economy. In the case of a developing economy like that of India the real task of facilitating agricultural growth consists in seeking to reduce the incidence of risk itself. Of course, this task of reducing the risk is a cooperative enterprise of both the Government—Central and State and the whole range of Panchayati Raj institutions on the one hand, and lending institutions like commercial and cooperative banks and NABARD on the other. That is, all lending institutions become partners in this task of risk réduction and it should be the business of these lending institutions to so devise their lending policies that their end result is not only growth-enhancing but also risk-reducing. Collectively, therefore, lending institutions would seek to change the risk profile of the agricultural sector as a whole. Do not be content with merely interpreting the existing risk but seek to change it. This motivation lends an entirely different perspective to our basic approach to lending. Viewed in this context, the present practice discussed earlier, of assessing the existing risk and building a premium into lending rates to agriculture, becomes flawed both in theory and practice, as spelt out earlier.

Looking at risks in agriculture either from the point of view of an individual farming unit, or from the viewpoint of a lending institution—both these are micro perceptions and this matrix is of limited relevance to situations in developing economies. We have already discussed the need to superimpose a macro perception on these two micro perceptions and thereby broaden the conceptual framework itself to suit the conditions in developing countries.

VI

RISK AND NON-PERFORMING ASSETS (NPAs)

During the phase of banking sector reforms in the 1990s, it became fashionable to use NPAs data, without appreciating the nuances characterising them, to give a bad name to certain sectors. Since NPAs were high in priority sectors, including agriculture, the incidence of risk was deemed to be high in these sectors. As the data presented in Table 1.1 show, 31 per cent of gross advance in priority sectors were NPAs in 1995. In contrast, in non-priority sectors the percentage of NPAs was low at 14. Hence, the conclusion drawn was that bankers should shy away from priority sectors; and that they should also add a risk premium to the lending rates of these sectors. Thus, NPAs were equated with the degrees of intrinsic risks in these sectors. It is legitimate to ask: How far is this interpretation justified?

Table 1.1

Sector-wise Proportion of Non-performing Advances of Public Sector Banks

(Rs. Crore)

Year	*Non-Priority Sector*		*Priority Sector*		*Total Advances*	
As at end (March)	*Gross Advances*	*Of which Non-performing Advances*	*Gross Advances*	*Of which Non-performing Advances*	*Gross Advances*	*Of which Non-performing Advances*
1995	135558	19177 *14.15*	61794	19208 *31.08*	197351	38385 *19.45*
1996	161712	22555 *13.95*	69609	19106 *27.45*	231321	41661 *18.01*
1997	165083	22803 *13.81*	79131	20774 *26.25*	244214	43577 *17.84*
1998	193652	24469 *12.64*	91319	21184 *23.20*	284971	45653 *16.02*
1999	218128	29103 *13.34*	107200	22607 *21.09*	325328	51710 *15.89*
2000	252599	29581 *11.73*	127478	23713 *18.55*	380077	53295 *14.02*
2001	293018	27307 *9.3*	149116	24156 *16.2*	442134	51463 *11.6*
2002	338184	30251 *8.9*	171185	25139 *14.7*	509369	55390 *10.9*
2003	374718	26781 *7.1*	203095	24938 *12.3*	577813	51720 *9.0*

Note: Figures in Italic are percentage of NPAs to Gross Advances.

Source: *Report on Trend and Progress of Banking in India* (various volumes).

To equate mechanistically NPAs with the incidence of intrinsic risks would be flawed. First, the dimensions of NPAs to priority sectors have to be judged in the historical perspective, as we have discussed earlier, of erosion of repayment ethics. Second, the neglect of priority sectors including agriculture by bankers during the 1990s must have also meant, neglect of follow-up of repayment of loans particularly of loans to small farmer borrowers. The disenfranchisement of small farmers, referred to earlier, must have also blown up the dimensions of NPAs.

This analysis is further strengthened by the more recent trend of a sharp decline in NPAs in priority sectors. For instance, NPAs in priority sectors declined from 31 per cent of gross advances in 1995 to 12 per cent in 2003. Even within the priority sectors, it is the small-scale industries' sub-sector which accounts for the bulk of NPAs in 2003, the NPAs of this sub-sector stood at 19 per cent. In contrast, the NPAs of agricultural sector stood at 10.5 per cent, declining from 13.7 per cent in 2001 (Table 1.2).

Table 1.2

Sub-sectorwise Proportion of Non-performing Asset to Gross Advances under Priority Sector in Public Sector Banks

(In Per Cent)

As at end March	*Agriculture*	*Small-scale Industries*	*Others*	*Total*
2001	13.7	21.3	15.9	16.2
2002	12.3	21.2	12.5	14.7
2003	10.5	19.2	9.9	12.3

A more encouraging feature of recent developments is that the trend in default is pronouncedly low in the case of incremental NPAs under advances under priority sectors. Out of the total NPAs, the share of priority sector NPAs has declined from 50 per cent in 1995 to 46 per cent in 1998, clearly reflecting a decline in incremental priority sector advances. The ratio of incremental NPAs to incremental advances was 6.7 per cent in the case of priority sector advances, as compared to 7.3 per cent for non-priority sectors.[25] In other words, a large chunk of the overhang of NPAs in the priority sector, including agriculture, was perhaps the result of inadequate appraisal, monitoring and follow-up of rural lending. With the improvement in the governance of banks, NPAs in priority sectors, including agriculture, are bound to decline further.

The point that is sought to be made, here, is that the dimensions of NPAs in a particular sector cannot be mechanistically interpreted as reflecting the intrinsic risks in the particular sector. One has to go behind the data to derive any policy conclusions.

25. Dadhich, G.L. (2001). *Directed Lending - A Critique,* Bank Economists' Concerence.

VII

GROWTH IMPERATIVES AND THE ROLE OF RURAL CREDIT

To reiterate, our risk philosophy must be firmly anchored in development imperatives. How does one translate this basic tenet into policy measures? First of all, we should have a clear vision of the profile of the future growth of the economy say, during the next decade or so. Secondly, rural credit policy would have to be shaped in such a way as to facilitate the growth pattern so envisaged.

Before spelling out, in concrete terms, the policy measures of such an approach, the need for debriefing bankers, particularly public sector bankers, about the new banking culture they have acquired during the 1990s should be underlined. It should be dinned into their ears that lending to priority sectors, including agriculture, is as important as lending to corporate elites, or capital market related activities or to consumer durables, or exports, or to housing. NPAs, as they have emerged historically, cannot be equated with intrinsic risks in the relevant sector; do not use these historical data of NPAs to shun some sectors. Policymakers of the 1990s brought up on the diet of IMF/World Bank market theology should, on their part, realise that their case for shunning subsidies to agriculture is flawed. The obscenely high level of subsidies entrenched in agriculture in developed countries should disabuse the minds of these policymakers of the anti-subsidy syndrome. The exhortation of these policymakers to Indian agriculture to be internationally competitive should be tempered by this basic fact. We need not be apologetic about extending subsidies to agriculture, including interest rate subsidy, wherever such subsidy is justified.

On the positive side, let us begin with the following statement of the Tenth Plan: "Agricultural development must be viewed as a core element of the Plan, since growth in this sector is likely to lead to the widest spread of benefits especially to the rural poor. The first generation of reforms concentrated on the industrial economy and reforms in the agricultural sector were neglected. This must change in the Tenth Plan."[26] The broad contours of the future growth of the economy, the critical role that agriculture would play in sustaining a GDP growth of 8 per cent or

26. *Tenth Five Year Plan, 2002-2007*, Vol. I, p. 9.

so, in ensuring food security and generating employment opportunities are spelt out clearly in the section IX.

On the whole, larger flow of credit alone can support higher agricultural growth, accelerated production of foodgrains, and decentralised growth.

The profile of future growth warrants that the rural credit system would have to take on, as it were, a new avatar not only in terms of diversification of loan-portfolio but also in terms of the architecture of the credit delivery mechanism. Rural credit will have to look well beyond crop loans.

Fresh water has emerged as a key constraint on future agricultural growth, because of the tightening supply and rapid expansion of demand. The present Government has realised the critical importance of water: "Water is the lifeline of civilisations. We have been warned that the biggest crisis that the World will face in the 21st century will be crisis of water."[27]

The idea of water as a precious resource which should carry a price tag, and the need for integrated water resources management at the community, state and national levels have now become the core of water-policy thinking. This is in consonance with the trend world over. "Even between the second World Water Forum held in 2000 in the Hague and the third held in 2003 in Kyoto, ideas had changed. Instead of compartmentalising 'water for health', 'water for food', and 'water for environment' a more holistic goal is in sight: water security and sanitation for all, especially for the poor."[28] In fact Dr. M.S. Swaminathan defines food security as, "physical, economic, social and ecological access to balanced diet, and clean drinking water for all and for ever." Viewed in this broader context, there is need for a decentralised approach to water harvesting and saving technologies, and equitably water-sharing methodologies based on soil and climatic condition on the one hand, and socio-cultural factors on the other.

Three inter-connected programmes assume prominence in this context: watershed development programmes; renovation of all the water bodies linked to agriculture, which have presently fallen into disuse; and rain water harvesting. Today, watershed development is seen as the principal

---

27. Chidambaram, P. (2004). "Budget Speech of Minister of Finance", July 8.
28. Black, Maggie and Rupert Talbot (2005). *Water: A Matter of Life and Health*, Oxford University Press, New Delhi, p. 240.

strategy for holistic development of rainfed areas, though in the initial stages it was conceived mainly as a measure for moisture conservation and soil stabilisation. The new 'Watershed Plus' approach to watershed development as spelt out in the Tenth Plan seeks to ensure convergence of all other programmes that promote economic activities and generate increased employment opportunities. Watershed development, both macro and micro, should have emerged as a major programme of agricultural and rural development. But even in Maharashtra, which is a pioneer in this area, only 15 per cent of the potential eligible area is covered by such programmes. Second, Indian agriculture has been historically sustained by natural and manmade water bodies such as tanks, lakes, ponds and similar structures. There are more than a million such structures, of which about 50,000 are utilised for irrigation. Many of them have fallen into disuse, accumulating silt and these need to be restored urgently. The Budget for 2004-05 proposes a massive scheme to repair, renovate and restore all these water bodies directly linked to agriculture. A pilot project one in each district would be launched straightaway at an estimated outlay of Rs. 100 crore. This is indeed a good beginning in an entirely neglected area. Thirdly, rainwater conservation and harvesting has important implications for the groundwater crisis that India is currently facing due to indiscriminate use of tube-well technology in different parts of the country. For rainwater harvesting to be effective, careful attention must be paid to the uses to which the water is put.

The thrust of policy in the coming years should, therefore, be on these three inter-connected programmes which, taken together, would go a considerable way towards reducing the degree of vulnerability of Indian agriculture to drought and thereby enhancing the sustainability of agricultural production at high levels and also food security. These provide an ideal example of risk-reducing and growth-enhancing avenues of credit deployment. Of course, the major support to these programmes might come from public and private investment but such investments need complementary support of rural credit, long, medium and short-term. There is some merit in rural credit institutions themselves taking initiatives in exploring such avenues for credit deployment. This holds true for both public sector banks and cooperative credit institutions. Also, there is a strong case for providing concessional lending rates to these segments because credit plays the dual role of growth enhancement and risk-reduction.

At this point, reference may be made to an important related issue, namely, promoting water use efficiency. Our water use efficiency in agriculture is perhaps the lowest in the world. Water use under different cropping systems and agro-climatic situations needs to be studied in-depth with a view to promoting economic and environmental efficiency. We need to promote on a large scale micro-irrigation technology through drip and sprinkler irrigation systems.

The refrain of the theme is that in the next couple of years lending of banks, cooperative credit institutions, and RRBs should be water-centric.

NABARD with its vast network of regional offices in all the State headquarters and its offices in most of the districts is ideally suited to take initiatives in providing a big boost to such water-centric programmes or projects. For instance, NABARD in collaboration with State Governments and panchayati raj institutions could organise the preparation of a blue-print for micro watershed development and related projects for all districts—in arid zones. The year say 2006 could be designated as a "Year of Water Resource Regeneration" for the purpose of implementing simultaneously this cluster of project. NABARD could also coordinate the financing of these projects by involving, wherever suitable PSBs, cooperative credit institutions and RRBs. In a way, NABARD could underwrite the financing of these projects in the sense that any shortfalls in resources could be met by it either directly or indirectly. Such a major thrust to water-centric programmes would go a considerable way towards changing the risk profile of agricultural sector, besides encouraging economic activities in the rural areas.

While on this subject, one analytical point needs to be underlined. It can be seen that the focus of risk management in agriculture is enlarged to cover not only crop production but also augmentation of water supplies for crop production. Viewed in this broader perspective the relevance of risk management models in agriculture, borrowed from developed countries, becomes seriously circumscribed.

There is a wide range of activities which have a direct or indirect bearing on agricultural and rural development. Some of these are elaborated in Part II: among them mention is made of organic farming with organic seed and compost preparation: utilisation of wastelands and development of forests. Most of these thrust areas of rural development, as envisaged in the Tenth Plan need credit support and hence the loan-portfolios of rural credit institutions should begin to reflect a more diversified credit support extended to these emerging areas. In a wider context, it has now become necessary to talk in terms of, what the recent Committee on Capital Formation in Agriculture, calls, "Capital Formation for Agriculture", in contrast to our conventional approach, of "Capital Formation in Agriculture". To quote the Committee's Report: "As agriculture is getting diversified, there is a need to not only augment but also restructure the pattern of investment in agriculture. Historically, the public sector has taken a lead in directing the growth and pattern of agricultural investment. We recommend that immediate steps should be taken to improve capital formation for agriculture in both public and private sectors. Otherwise, it may be difficult to sustain the agricultural growth and rural purchasing power. Currently, irrigation accounts for the bulk of public investment (above 90 per cent). The new strategy of agricultural growth and diversification of agriculture from traditional crop cultivation to horticulture, etc. would require more investment in cold storage, rural roads, communication, marketing network and facilities, warehouses, etc. Simultaneously, efforts should be made to revitalise agriculture through introduction of biotechnology and other innovations. This would require substantial increase in investment in research and development for agriculture."[29]

Let us now turn to the other facet of the new avatar, namely, the transformation of the credit delivery mechanism. Underlying the present sickness of the rural credit system are two core causes: high transaction costs and poor recovery performance. More recent experience has demonstrated that both these problems can be tacked effectively through the instrumentality of micro credit institutions. The experiment of micro finance through the conduit of SHGs has shown that transaction costs could be reduced drastically and repayment rates can be as high as 90 per cent. Incidentally, this shows that NPAs do not reflect intrinsic risks in lending to agriculture. Both RBI and NABARD have been recently spearheading the promotion and linkage of SHGs to the banking system through refinance support and other proactive policies. The programme initiated in 1992 covered, at the end of March 2003, 31,000 rural outlets of more than 500 banks, with loan portfolio of Rs. 2,000 crore. Thus, the programme has enabled the formal banking system to reach 11.6 million poor households through the conduit of 7.17 lakh SHGs. But we have a long way to go to be able to cover the bulk of the rural poor families. In any case, the role of micro credit as an appropriate institutional instrument to reduce credit risks, as perceived by bankers, is now established and the rural credit system—commercial banks, cooperatives and RRBs—must move towards spreading this model, and spreading it fast.

29. Government of India (2003). *Report of the Committee on Capital Formation in Agriculture*, New Delhi, March, p. 21.

Overall, it is clear that production risk in agriculture could be reduced through the schemes like watershed development discussed earlier. The repayment risk could be reduced through evolving a new architecture of the rural credit delivery mechanism. Taken together these reforms would go a long way towards changing the risk profile of the agricultural sector as a whole.

VIII

PRICE RISKS AND CROP INSURANCE

At the end, a brief reference may be made, as a postscript to the main theme, to two risk protection measures, namely, price support and crop insurance.

Price Support

The current debate questions the utility of the food security system in the context of ongoing liberalisation of trade in foodgrains and the comfortable foreign exchange reserves position. It may be recalled that to protect farmers from the risk of wide fluctuations in the price of farm products, Government has been providing, for some years, Minimum Support Prices (MSP) for 24 major crops including paddy, wheat, *jowar*, *bajra*, maize, *ragi*, pulses, oilseeds, copra, cotton, jute, sugarcane and tobacco.[30] In the case of rice and wheat in particular, this incentive mechanism—the MSP, procurement of foodgrains by Food Corporation of India (FCI) and public distribution of foodgrains—has worked wonders for the supply scenario. India which was a chronic importer of foodgrains in the 1960s—imports of wheat averaged 3 million tonnes per year—has been transformed into one of the major foodgrains exporters today. India exported 10 million tonnes of rice and wheat in 2003-04. Assured minimum prices for rice and wheat, over the years, have promoted investment in the production of these crops and facilitated sustained growth. The system has created, in its wake, however, some distortions like distorted cropping pattern, burgeoning foodgrains stocks and mounting food subsidies. As a consequence, and inspired by the market theology, there is clamour by some sections, for abolition of the whole incentive mechanism. "The disgrace is that MSP has not been slashed, as

30. Government of India, *Economic Survey* 2003-04, p. 92.

it ought to have been."[31] This is not an appropriate place for an in-depth analysis of the whole issue. The limited point, relevant to our main theme, which needs to be driven home is: market theologists should be warned of the grave dangers to food security, if this incentive mechanism is dismantled on the specious ground of 'surpluses' of foodgrains. Our contemporary policy makers should, first, disabuse their minds of this illusion of 'surpluses'. What we have now is a situation of an 'effective demand surplus' and not a genuine surplus. The task of meeting future foodgrains requirements looks formidable. Even modest projections of demand for cereals in 2020 place the estimate at 260 million tonnes, as compared to the production level of 210 million tonnes in 2003-04. The enormous gap to be bridged between demand and supply is obvious, especially in the context of production in the more fertile, well-endowed lands having reached a sort of plateau. Secondly, we are only too familiar with the rapacious nature of private trade in foodgrains. Private trade's strategy of exploiting both farmers and consumers by depressing prices in the post-harvest period and artificially raising them in the lean season is now part of the folklore of textbooks on the Indian economy. Left to private trade, foodgrains' prices especially of wheat, would have crashed in the years of glut: for instance, when foodgrains' stocks with FCI reached a peak of 60 million tonnes. This would have had the adverse impact on medium-term production trend of these crops. Similarly, in the years of severe drought as in the case of 2002-03, foodgrains prices would have sky-rocketed.

The fact that neither crash nor spurt in prices took place in reality is a vindication of the effectiveness of the incentive mechanism built up over the years. Against this background, dismantling the incentive mechanism would tantamount to throwing the baby away with the bath water. To argue on these lines is certainly not to deemphasis the importance of streamlining the MSP mechanism, or the efforts to improve the efficiency of FCI operations. The limited point that is sought to be made is that assured minimum prices for main foodgrains should continue to form an essential ingredient in the policy-mix designed to promote sustained production of foodgrains.

Crop Insurance

Crop insurance basically protects the farmer from weather induced risks like flood, drought, hailstorms, etc. and price risks. As RBI has

31. "Rethink Food Strategy", Editorial in *Economic Times*, November 6, 2004.

emphasised recently, "To attain higher growth in agriculture, the major areas requiring attention in the financial sector are, *inter alia* spread of insurance against crops..."[32]

There was a Comprehensive Crop Insurance Scheme (CCIS) in operation since 1985. In its place, Government of India introduced a new scheme entitled "National Agricultural Insurance Scheme" (NAIS) from the *rabi* 1999-2000 season. The scheme is available to all farmers irrespective of their size of land holdings. It envisages coverage of all the food crops (cereals, millets and pulses), oilseeds and annual commercial and horticultural crops, in respect of which past data are available for an adequate number of years.

The premium rates are 3.5 per cent of the sum insured for *bajra* and oilseed, 2.5 per cent for other *kharif* crops, 1.5 per cent for wheat, and 2 per cent for other *rabi* crops. Small and medium farmers are entitled to a subsidy of 50 per cent of the premium which is shared on 50:50 basis by the Central and State Governments. The premium subsidy is expected to be phased out over a period of 5 years.

The scheme is operating on the basis of 'Area Approach', that is, defined areas for each notified crop for widespread calamities and on 'an individual basis' for localised calamities like hailstorm, landslide, cyclone and flood. At present the scheme is being implemented in 23 States and 2 Union Territories.[33]

Data regarding the area and farmers covered, the sum insured, insurance charges, etc. are provided in the following Table 1.3.

It is, thus, clear that in terms of overall dimensions involved, the coverage is limited. A more basic question is: how far such insurance is economically viable? Examining cross country experiences with crop insurance. Dr. Bhupat Desai sums up the situation: "coverage is limited, implementation is fraught with managerial difficulties and moral hazards, and crop insurance programme is financially unviable and a drain on public exchequer."[34] These studies showed, for instance, that to fully recover the cost of this programme in a country like the USA, the premium would have to be as high as 20 per cent!

---

32. Reserve Bank of India, *Annual Report, 2003-04*, p. 117.
33. Government of India (2004). *Economic Survey, 2003-04*, p. 162 and 167.
34. Desai, Bhupat M. (1989). "Is Crop Insurance An Answer to India's Agricultural Development?" *Nirnay*, September.

Table 1.3

Performance of the National Agricultural Insurance Scheme

Sr. No.	*Particulars*	*Rabi 2000-01*	*Kharif 2001*	*Rabi 2001-02*	*Kharif 2002*	*Rabi 2002-03*	*Kharif 2003*	*Total*
1.	Farmers Covered (in lakh)	20.92	86.96	19.55	97.65	23.27	79.69	328.04
2.	Sum Insured (Rs. in crore)	1,602.68	7,502.46	1,497.51	9,429.44	1,837.53	8,110.13	29,979.75
3.	Insurance Charges (Rs. in crore)	27.79	261.62	30.15	325.38	38.50	283.14	966.58
4.	Area Coverage (in lakh ha)	31.11	128.88	31.46	155.22	40.38	122.89	509.94
5.	Total Claims (Rs. in crore)	59.49	492.63	64.66	1,821.79	193.03	191.92	2,823.52
6.	Claims Paid (Rs. in crore)	59.25	492.32	64.37	1,754.28	114.15	12.02	2,496.39

Source: *Economic Survey*, 2003-04, p. 163.

Perhaps, selectively, crop insurance schemes could be tried in specific circumstances; but they cannot provide total solution to the general question of risk protection of farmers.

We cannot do better than sum up the current situation in the following words of Dr. Y.V. Reddy, Governor, RBI: "...On the critical issue of risk-mitigation, it is held that experiments with crop or credit-insurance in India have not been very satisfactory so far. In fact, many farmers argue that where compulsory insurance is resorted to, it increases the burden of borrowing from institutional sources and once the transaction costs are added, the overall costs exceed the Prime Lending Rates Significantly.... Perhaps, it is necessary to recognise that if some elements of insurance are *ab initio* not viable, extending credit becomes more risky and hence constrainted."[35]

35. Reddy, Y.V. (2004). "Rural Credit: Status and Agenda", *Reserve Bank of India Bulletin*, December.

IX

AGRICULTURE AND INDIA'S ECONOMIC DEVELOPMENT: MACRO PERCEPTIONS

Role and Relevance of Priority Sector Lending in a Globalised Banking Scenario

In the recent economic history of India, the 1990s would go down as a lost decade for priority sectors including agriculture, and for the poor who constitute more than a quarter of the total population. Policymakers both at the Central Government and at the RBI, soaked in the market theology of the IMF and World Bank version, succeeded in shifting the focus of macroeconomic management away from the end-objectives of development, namely, reduction in poverty and improvement in the quality of life of the bulk of the population. The poor practically disappeared from the development agenda and the policymakers seemed to stipulate: let the poor fend for themselves. This was especially unfortunate because Indian policymakers were pioneers in emphasising the distributive aspects of growth right from the inception of planning in 1951, at a time when it was not fashionable in development economics to do so. There was in the 1990s, an amazing perversion of priorities. Privatisation was pursued with a missionery zeal, with the Minister for Disinvestment emerging as a messiah of modern capitalist India. The other obsessive concerns were development of the Capital market and the import of gold. Throwing open portfolio investment to foreign institutional investors (FIIs), extending fiscal concessions to investment in equity and a host of other supportive measures were taken to boost the capital market. RBI winked at the defaults of PSBs in terms of their adhering to the credit targets set for priority sectors and agriculture; and at the same time goaded PSBs to involve themselves increasingly in the capital market, both directly and indirectly. Import of gold was liberalised with a vengeance, the average annual imports soaring to staggering level of $ 5 billion. Policymakers pleaded paucity of resources when it was a question of additional investment in irrigation, but they had no compunction to release resources of the alarming dimensions for investment in an unproductive asset like gold. Fortunately, we were able to produce reasonably adequate quantities of foodgrains but by the mindless pursuit of flawed food management policies, inspired by market theology; we allowed foodgrains stocks with the public sector to accumulate to more than 60 million tonnes.

Substantial reduction in food subsidies inspired by market theology, resulted in foodgrains becoming increasingly inaccessible to the poor and as a consequence, offtake of foodgrains from the public distribution system (PDS) declined sharply. Food mountain, thus, coexisted with a distressingly large proportion of underfed and undernourished population. Policymakers in their wisdom found a brilliant solution to the food mountain: export foodgrains with a substantial subsidy, no matter market theology does not permit subsidisation for domestic consumption ! Exports of rice and wheat soared to 10 million tonnes in 2002-03. The Economic Survey, 2003-04 exults in this achievement: "Agricultural exports increased from $5.9 billion in 2001-02 to $ 6.7 billion in 2002-03...The exports of foodgrains (rice and wheat) have picked up considerably in recent years accounting for around 20 per cent of the agricultural exports. The Government's special efforts to encourage exports of foodgrains in recent years through grant of WTO compatible subsidies has placed India as one of the leading exporters of foodgrains in the international market."[36] Is this the impact of globalisation on the Indian economy? India is the abode of the largest number of underfed and undernourished population in the world. It is tragic enough not to be able to produce adequate quantities of foodgrains to meet domestic consumption requirements: it is a greater tragedy that we are unwilling to utilise all the foodgrains produced for domestic consumption. In any other country, such massive exports of foodgrains against the background of chronic semi-starvation would have exploded into a revolution. But ours is an ancient civilisation known for its quiescence. Food security in a meaningful sense is ensured by not merely producing an adequate quantum of foodgrains but also by ensuring that the grains so produced do reach the needy. In fact the Tenth Plan should have devoted a whole chapter to find an appropriate solution to the problem of evolving a food delivery mechanism which would ensure food security in a holistic sense.

Overall, the interregnum of 12 or 13 years since 1991 to 2003 remains a nightmare in India's development dream.

It was left to the UPA Government to rediscover, as it were, poverty in 2004: its National Common Minimum Programme (NCMP) reflects this rediscovery: "Empowering the people especially the poor with universal access to education and health, and facilitating their full participation in the growth process through gainful employment will enhance their welfare. It will reinforce the growth process itself. This win-win strategy is the key

36. Government of India (2004). *Economic Survey, 2003-04*, p. 106.

stone of the economic policy framework of the Government."[37] One of the seven important economic objectives[38] spelt out in this context is: assuring 100 days's employment to the breadwinner in each family at the minimum wage. Implementation of these programmes, however, is not going to be an easy task. The corrosive influence of market theology nurtured by economic reforms during the 13 years interregnum is reflected in the new banking culture which shuns lending to priority sectors or to small borrowers generally; and in the new governance culture which has become almost insensitive to poverty and its attendant evils. Changing the mindsets of the actors involved in the financial and development sectors, and re-orienting the policy thrusts pose a great challenge to the development today. This would also mean redefinition of our basic approach to poverty reduction and re-drafting our development agenda. All this would involve, to borrow the words of Prime Minister Dr. Manmohan Singh: "a change in the manner in which the country is run, a change in the national priorities and the change in the processes and focus of governance."[39] It may be reiterated that priority sectors would continue to play a critical role in the growth and development of the Indian economy, not withstanding its globalisation. The financial system, particularly PSBs will have to readdress themselves to the task of lending credit support to this role. To enable the PSBs to do so, it may be necessary to debrief bankers about the new banking culture they have acquired under the delusions of globalised banking. In the new milieu, rural credit will have to take on a new *avatar*, both in terms of diversification of loan portfolio and in terms of the credit delivery mechanism.

New Avatar of Rural Credit

The resurrection of rural credit would also necessarily warrant that the system should take on, as it were, a new *Avatar* not only in terms of diversification of loan-portfolio, but also in terms of the credit delivery mechanism. Underlying the present sickness of the rural credit system are two core causes: high transaction costs and poor recovery performance. More recent experience has demonstrated that both these problems can be tackled effectively through the instrumentality of micro credit institutions. The experiment of micro finance through the conduit of SHGs has shown that transaction costs could be reduced drastically and repayment rates can

---

37. Chidambaram, P. (2004). "Budget Speech of Finance Minister", 8th July.

38. Quoted by Finance Minister in his Budget Speech referred to in footnote 37.

39. Mujumdar, N.A. (2002). *Financial Sector Reforms and India's Economic Development*, Volume 1 and 2. Academic Foundation, Delhi; and also Mujumdar, N.A. (2004). *Economic Reforms Sans Development*, Academic Foundation, Delhi.

be as high as 90 per cent. Both RBI and NABARD have been recently spear heading the promotion and linkage of SHGs to the banking system through refinance support and other proactive policies. Three models of credit linkage of SHGs with banks have emerged. SHGs formed and financed by banks; and SHGs financed by banks using NGOs as financial intermediaries. The programme initiated in 1992 covers, 31,000 rural outlets of more than 500 banks, with a loan portfolio of Rs. 2,000 crore (end-March 2003). Thus the programme has enabled the formal banking system to reach 11.6 million poor households through the conduit of 7.17 lakh SHGs.[40] The role of micro-credit as the most appropriate and economically feasible alternative in attaining the objectives of both growth and poverty alleviation is thus well established and the rural credit system—commercial banks, cooperatives and RRBs—must move towards spreading this model, and spreading it fast. The coverage of poor families today is modest: only 11.6 million poor families out of the total of some 58 million. Secondly, uneven growth of micro finance in terms of regional distribution. As at the end of March 2003, of the total SHGs credit linked, Andhra Pradesh accounted for nearly 40 per cent. Taking the four states Andhra Pradesh, Karnataka, Tamil Nadu and Uttar Pradesh, together, they accounted for nearly 70 per cent of total SHGs credit—linked and 80 per cent of the total amount of bank loans.

This model of reaching rural credit to different segments of the rural sector through the instrumentality of NGOs or SHGs should be replicated in States other than these mentioned above. Of course, NABARD has been playing a catalytic role both in terms of promotional grant support to NGOs and nurturing SHGs. But this is not enough. PSBs, on their part should also make similar efforts to promote and nurture NGOs and SHGs: because, as we have seen earlier, such efforts would be mutually beneficial both to the lending institution and the beneficiaries of bank credit. But one looks in vain for such initiatives in the "Banking Industry Vision 2010" document prepared by the Indian Banks' Association (IBA). It is unfortunate that document does not even take consizance of the problems of rural branches, of inability to meet the target for agricultural credit, despite low credit-deposit ratios. For the IBA, God is in heaven and everything is alright with rural credit. The document is content with mouthing empty rhetories about market theology. The banking system is expected to reorient its approach to rural lending. 'Going Rural' could be the new market *mantra*. Rural market comprises 74 per cent of the

40. *Banking Industry Vision 2010*, Indian Banks' Association, November 2003, pp. 42-43.

population, 41 per cent of Middle class and 58 per cent of disposable income .... Banks' approach to the rural lending will be guided mainly by commercial considerations in future .... Rural financial system (should) emerge as "one stop destination" for all types of credit requirements of people in rural/semi-urban centers."[41] This is another instance of the new banking culture fostered by banking sector reforms. RBI and NABARD will therefore have to sensitise PSBs to participate actively in their endeavour to bring the micro credit into the mainstream of the rural financial system. On its part, IBA seems to be bereft of ideas. In contrast, look at initiatives that a high profile private sector bank ICICI Bank—which has engaged a super-star as its brand ambassador at a hefty fee—has taken recently to widen its rural reach. ICICI Bank has entered into agreement with Micro-credit Foundation of India (MFI), which is involved with some 10,000 SHGs in Tamil Nadu. Under the agrement MFI would extend finance for income-generating activities of the SHGs, which are expected to need about Rs. 1,250 crore which ICICI Bank will lend through MFI. There is some risk sharing between ICICI Bank and MFI. ICICI plans to have similar tie-ups with other micro-finance institutions in other parts of the country.[42]

The problem with the cooperative credit institutions is not merely one of infusion of capital, which is no doubt necessary: but also of governance and professional management. The cooperative movement has lost its *elan* of yesteryears and today it lacks a sense of direction. The NPAs of urban cooperative banks are as high as 21 per cent. In fact the share of cooperative credit institutions in total rural finance has declined in recent years. The role of cooperative credit sector needs to be redefined in the context of financial sector reforms. Cooperative credit institutions particularly at the district level should also promote SHGs or utilise NGOs for their credit deployment. In other words, by adopting a similar paradigm of credit deployment as the bank-linked SHGs, cooperative credit institutions should be able to improve their overall performance, in terms of reducing transaction costs, improving repayment performance and reducing NPAs.

There is yet another dimension to the new paradigm of credit development. Panchayati Raj institutions are playing a major role in rural development at least in some States. For instance, in West Bengal and Kerala about 40 per cent of the annual plan outlay is disbursed through

41. See: *Hindu Business Line*, March 10, 2004.

42. "Rural Development: New Perceptions", *Economic and Political Weekly*, September 28, 2002.

Panchayati Raj institutions. Commercial and Cooperative banks should 'begin to look at viable projects sponsored by Panchayati Raj institutions. Lending to these institutions may also help to reduce transaction costs and improve repayment performance.

Good Governance

Good governance in rural financial institutions is a critical determinant of the success of rural development programmes. Today availability of resources is not acting as a constraint on larger flow of rural credit but inefficient management. Commercial banks have been highly liquid for the last decade or so and yet they have not succeeded in meeting the credit target for agriculture. Secondly, take the case of utilisation of funds under Rural Infrastructure Development Fund (RIDF). The Fund was originally set up with NABARD in 1995-96 with a corpus of Rs. 2,000 crore with the major objective of providing funds, to state governments to enable them to complete ongoing infrastructure projects pertaining to irrigation, flood protection, rural roads and bridges. The scope of RIDF has been progressively widened to include lending to *Gram Panchayats*, Self-Help Groups for implementing village level infrastructure projects. Although, the total corpus under RIDF adds up to Rs. 34,000 crore as of 2002-03, the overall utilisation of these funds is dismal at 58 per cent. In fact, the percentage of utilisation declined to 40 and 18 per cent in 2002 and 2003. Are the reconnaissance efforts of NABARD to identify eligible projects unsatisfactory? Or, are the States indifferent to rural development? One begins to wonder.

Take another example of rural administration. The Food-for-Work Programme was started in 2000-01 aiming at augmenting food security through wage employment. Foodgrains were supplied to States, under this programme, free of cost. Unfortunately, the record of lifting of foodgrains allotted for the scheme from the Food Corporation of India (FCI) has been very disappointing. For instance, against the allocation of 35.31 lakh tonnes of foodgrains, only 21.26 lakh tonnes were lifted by target states up to January 2002. Was the Centre not persuasive enough? Or, do the States need to be sensitised about the misery of poverty, unemployment and the state of semi-starvation?

This case is particularly relevant, if we want to utilise the huge surpluses of foodgrains with FCI for rural development. A scheme of 'grain loans' could be devised by which all financial institutions involved in rural development could augment their financial resources by drawing on such 'grain loans', from FCI.

Financial Sector reforms introduced in the 1990s created an adversarial environment for rural credit, as a result of which the rural credit system finds itself in a moribund state today. As the economy enters the third year of the Tenth Plan, the configuration of circumstances is such as to warrant the resurrection of rural credit. To facilitate inclusive, or, broad-based and decentralised growth, the rural credit system would have to take on a new *Avatar*: the micro finance segment has to be integrated with the mainstream rural finance sector by appropriate linkages of banks/ cooperatives with SHGs and NGOs. Loan portfolio's of rural credit institutions would be more diversified by stretching their operations beyond the conventional crop loans, and transactions with Panchayati Raj Institutions would multiply. Good governance will be an important input to upgrade the efficiency of all financial institutions involved in rural development.

X

CONCLUDING OBSERVATIONS: AREAS WARRANTING ACTION

The main areas in which action is needed could be briefly summed as below:

1. At the outset there is a need to debrief public sector bankers about the new banking culture they have acquired during the financial sector reforms phase of the 1990s. It should be dinned into the ears of these bankers that lending to agriculture and related sectors, as spelt out in this paper, is as important as lending to the three "Cs"—corporate elite, consumer durables and capital market related activities. Fortunately, the NCMP of the UPA Government has already gone someway towards changing the mindsets of bankers. Both RBI and NABARD could impress upon PSBs that priority sectors would continue to be critical in India's future growth and development.

2. The present guidelines issued by RBI on risk assessment and management are inappropriate for agriculture and rural sectors generally. RBI jointly with NABARD could set up a working group to evolve, in the light of the risk philosophy outlined in this paper, appropriate guidelines for rural lending by commercial banks, cooperative credit institutions and RRBs. The guidelines should,

among others, identify agriculture and related sectors or sub-sectors to which credit—short, medium, and long-term—needs to be extended. There should be prioritisation among sectors and sub-sectors for the purpose of identifying those that deserve concessional lending. The PSBs should diversify their loan portfolio by extending their reach to a whole range of sub-sectors discussed in this paper. This is one aspect of the new avatar that the rural credit system has to take to meet the new challenges. The second aspect of the avatar is the new architecture of the credit delivery system. The preferred mode of lending to different sectors or sub-sectors—either directly or through NGOs and SHGs—may also be spelt out.

3. The guidelines should also stress the proactive role that bank and other lending institutions should play in translating the enormous potential demand for institutional credit in the rural sector into effective demand. They should explore and identify such potential demand for credit and assist in giving a concrete shape to such demand by converting it into credit worthy projects. Several of the new segments discussed in the paper need such initiatives by bankers. Rural credit expansion has to be, as in the past, supply-led and not so much demand-derived.

4. In the immediate future rural lending should be water-centric. In fact the concept of food security has been recently widened to include access to adequate water. Three inter-connected programmes have been discussed in the paper: watershed development programme, both micro and macro, renovation of all the water bodies linked to agriculture, which have fallen into disuse presently; and promotion of rainwater harvesting and conservation technologies. Programmes designed to promote water use efficiency should also form an integral part of this exercise.

5. NABARD is ideally suited to take a lead in providing a big boost to such water-centric programmes. NABARD in collaboration with State Governments and Panchayati Raj institutions could organise the preparation of a blue print for micro watershed development and related projects in all the districts in the arid zone. The year 2006 could be designated as the 'Year of Water Resource Regeneration' for the purpose of implementing simultaneously this cluster of projects. NABARD could coordinate the financing of these projects and in fact could underwrite these projects.

6. While production risk in agriculture could be reduced through water-centric programmes, repayment risks faced by rural lending institutions could be reduced through evolving a new architecture of the rural credit delivery mechanism. Both RBI and NABARD have been, in recent years, spearheading the promotion and linkage of SHGs to the banking system through refinance support and other proactive policies. Focus should be on spreading this model of rural financing and spreading it fast.

Part II

Agriculture and Inclusive Growth

2

Centrality of Agriculture to India's Economic Development

Indian agriculture has come a long way since the inception of planning in 1951. All along there was an almost obsessive concern for development policy with the attainment of self-sufficiency in food. This is perfectly understandable because we have lived with the nightmare of absolute shortage of foodgrains supplies in the 1960s, when the average annual imports of wheat hovered around three million tonnes. We survived through the munificence of the US, which supplied wheat to us under its PL480 programme. This donor-donee relationship was far from flattering, as revealed in the following quotation, reproduced by M.L. Dantwala, from the book *'Famine 1975!'* by Paddock Brothers.

"America will have to apply the classical medical 'triage' method. Like doctors in the battlefield trying to make the best out of minimum resources, she will have to decide which countries to save and which to sacrifice... . Today India absorbs, like a blotter, 25 per cent of the entire American wheat crop. No matter how one may adjust present statistics and allow for future increase in the American wheat crop...it will be beyond the resources of the US to keep famine out of India during the 1970s. The reason? Of all national leaderships, the Indian comes close to being the most childish and inefficient and perversely determined to cut the country's economic throat." The moral: If other more deserving countries are to be saved, India must be sacrificed.[1]

The founding fathers of the Indian Society of Agricultural Economics had in their wisdom inscribed in the Society's logo the following motto: "*Dhana Dhanyam Vipulam Bhavatu*", or, "Let there be surpluses of wealth and foodgrains." History has proved that their judgment was far more

1. Dantwala, M.L. (1972). "Preface" to the Proceedings of the International Seminar on *Comparative Experience of Agricultural Development in Developing Countries of Asia and the South East Since the Second World War*, Indian Society of Agricultural Economics.

percipient than the American perception reflected in the statement quoted above. Thanks to the green revolution, India attained self-sufficiency in foodgrains in the 1970s and what is more, has emerged as a major exporter of foodgrains in more recent years: Exports of rice and wheat soared to 10 million tonnes in 2002-03.

The Economic Survey 2003-2004 exults in this achievement: "Agricultural exports increased from $ 5.9 billion in 2001-02 to $ 6.7 billion in 2002-2003.... The exports of foodgrains (rice and wheat) have picked up considerably in recent years, accounting for around 20 per cent of the agricultural exports. The government's special efforts to encourage exports of foodgrains in recent years through grant of World Trade Organisation (WTO), compatible subsidies has placed India as one of the leading exporters of foodgrains in the international market."[2]

This transformation of Indian agriculture from a chronically shortage sector to the so-called 'surplus' sector, would have made a fascinating story, if only the problems facing Indian agriculture had evaporated, as it were, along with the foodgrains deficit. Alas, this is not so. Indian agriculture in the new millennium faces a far more complex set of problems though they are of a different genre. For instance, India remains the abode of the largest number of underfed and undernourished population in the world. According to FAO, over 225 million Indians remain chronically undernourished. How does one explain the apparent paradox of the coexistence of large 'surpluses' of foodgrains with a sizeable underfed and undernourished population? The export surpluses of foodgrains, of which the Economic Survey boasts, is an effective demand surplus and not a genuine surplus. It was tragic enough for a predominantly agricultural economy not to be able to produce in the 1960s, adequate quantities of foodgrains to meet the domestic consumption requirements of the population: it is perhaps a greater systemic tragedy today that even when we are able to produce adequate quantities of foodgrains, we are unable to ensure that the grains so produced do reach the needy. Food security in a meaningful sense is ensured by not merely producing an adequate quantum of foodgrains but also by ensuring their access to all those who are in need. This is the new dimension of food security, which development policies are now called upon to address in the new millennium.

Attainment of food self-sufficiency, even in a technical sense, is admittedly an important landmark in the history of growth of Indian

2. Government of India (2004). *Economic Survey, 2003-2004*, p. 106.

agriculture, but this has not meant the dilution of problems facing Indian agriculture. Problems of agricultural growth and rural development in general continue to remain, in the new millennium, as daunting as they were in the 1950s. One major difference is that agricultural sector today faces a host of what we might call second generation problems on which we would seek to focus.

As is well known, the share of agriculture in the total national income declined sharply from some 50 per cent in the 1950s to around 20 or 22 per cent in more recent years. Of course, this phenomenon of declining importance of agriculture is part of the process of development itself. The more developed an economy, the lower the contribution of agriculture to national income. In developed economies like the UK, for instance, agriculture accounts for hardly five per cent of national income.

What is perhaps unique about the Indian agricultural scenario is that despite the secular decline in its contribution to national income, the centrality of agricultural growth to Indian economic development cannot be de-emphasised. In the Indian economy, the importance of agriculture transcends its primary function of mere crop production. Agriculture continues to hold the key to higher GDP growth, employment expansion, reduction in poverty, and the equitable distribution of income. The larger than sectoral role of Indian agriculture stems from the basic fact that a large proportion of the population, some 60 per cent, continues to depend on agriculture for its livelihood. That is, despite the sustained growth of GDP of some 6 per cent in recent years, the non-agricultural sector has not been able to siphon off surplus labour from the agricultural sector. Nor is it likely to do so in the medium-term. This is in sharp contrast to the empirical experience of developed countries. It is this India-specific configuration of circumstances which places agricultural or rural development in general in a pre-eminent position in the development agenda.

Oblivious of these broader dimensions of agricultural growth, Indian policymakers of the 1990s, in the first flush of enthusiasm of liberalisation and globalisation of the Indian economy, neglected agriculture, with disastrous consequences. In part they were inspired by the market theology of the IMF and World Bank. Thus, the 1990s was a lost decade for agriculture: the rate of agricultural growth decelerated, investment and credit flow to the[3] rural sector shrank, and the rural credit delivery system

3. For a detailed discussion, Mujumdar, N.A. (2001). *The New Architecture of the Rural Credit System*, Mumbai University, Mumbai; and Mujumdar, N.A. (2004). "Resurrection of Rural Credit", *Bank Quest*, July-September.

became practically moribund. There was disenfranchisement of a large number of small farmers, as reflected in the sharp decline in the number of small borrowing accounts of banks. Manmohan Singh, the Prime Minister, admits: "What is alarming, however, is that there seems to have been a neglect of agriculture in the past decade."[4]

If we have to ensure a sustained growth of the economy of 7 to 8 per cent per annum in the coming years, agricultural growth will have to be stepped up to say, 4 per cent. In the 1990s, agricultural growth was less than 2 per cent per annum. The Tenth Plan assumes a growth rate of 4 per cent for the agriculture sector, but in reality, the average annual growth rate for the first three years of the Tenth Plan was hardly 1.5 per cent.

The imperatives of accelerated agricultural growth in the coming years are, thus, obvious. Perhaps what is more daunting is that economists would need to address the second generation problems. Which are far more complex. Merely ensuring faster agricultural growth is not enough, important though this objective is. The character of such growth is of equal concern. Our vision of agricultural growth in the new millennium would have to be that it should be a means of achieving the broader objectives of food security, employment-led growth and poverty reduction.[5]

Our strategy for future agricultural growth should be anchored in this broader vision. The twin objectives of accelerating agricultural growth and ensuring food security for all at the household level—we will discuss this aspect presently—warrants a new paradigm of development which is pro-poor, and pro-environment in terms of sustainability of growth. This strategy should ensure that higher growth is accompanied by a narrowing down of disparities in regional growth and of productivity differentials among different farm-size groups. This, in turn, implies that in future, greater emphasis should be placed on agriculture in rain-fed or dry regions, where there is concentration of poverty and food insecurity. Alongside large and medium irrigation projects, watershed development projects, both macro and micro, should be undertaken on a massive scale.

The issues underlying this strategy can be conveniently discussed under four broad heads: food security, employment, water resources and diversification of agriculture.

---

4. Singh, Manmohan (2005). "Second Green Revolution in Indian Agriculture", Address at Agriculture Summit 2005, *Economic Developments in India*, Vol. 89.

5. Desai, B.M. (2002). "Policy Framework for Re-orienting Agricultural Development", *Indian Journal of Agricultural Economics*, January-March.

Food Security

As mentioned at the outset, the transformation of the agrarian economy from one of acute scarcity into the so-called 'surplus' situation should not obscure the fact that a sizeable section of the population continues to remain underfed and undernourished. In the context of this paradox of surplus foodgrains coexisting with an underfed population, statements like, 'The country is self-sufficient in foodgrains' are reduced to empty rhetoric. This brings into focus the question of access to food in terms of not only physical access, in the sense of mere availability, but also economic access to food. Looked at from the household point of view, therefore, food security would have to be equated with livelihood security. The only way by which a poor household could be empowered with the purchasing power to access food is by way of providing a means of livelihood or employment, a subject we will discuss presently.

Recently, M.S. Swaminathan has added another dimension to food security. He defines food security as, "Livelihood security for the households and all members within, which ensures both physical and economic access to balanced diet, safe drinking water, environmental sanitation, primary education and basic healthcare."[6] Thus, providing drinking water for all has become an integral component of food security.

If it is possible to provide economic access to food to most of the poor, G.S. Bhalla[7] argues that India may have to import foodgrains to meet our requirements let alone seeking to export. In this context he makes a reference to China which, despite high growth in foodgrains production, has to import 12 to 13 million tonnes of foodgrains annually to meet its food and feed requirements.

Employment

If providing economic access to food through generation of employment is an effective way of ensuring food security to the poor, how does one go about expanding employment?

The current backlog of unemployment is around 9 per cent or equivalent to 35 million persons and this is far too high. Even if a 7 or 8 per cent GDP growth is sustained in the coming years, the organised sectors like large and medium industries including service sectors, IT

---

6. Swaminathan, M.S. (1996). "Science and Technology for Sustainable Food Security", *Indian Journal of Agricultural Economics*, January-June.

7. Bhalla, G.S. (1995). "Globalisation and Agricultural Policy", *Indian Journal of Agricultural Economics*, January-March.

sector, etc. can do precious little to clear this backlog and meet the demands for employment of the additions to the labour force. In other words, jobs generated autonomously by the normal growth process will fall far short of the requirement. The policy thrust will have to be, thus, necessarily on decentralised and broad-based growth. The focus will have to be on agriculture and allied sectors, like animal husbandry, fisheries, construction, tourism, small-scale industries (SSIs), micro-enterprises, retail trade, and so on. Agriculture is used here as an inclusive concept, which would also cover development of wastelands and forests, and organic farming, with organic seed and compost preparation. The critical relevance of the rural sector for food security is, thus, clear.

The only asset that the poor has is labour and perhaps one way of empowering the poor to access foodgrains is through providing employment. The National Rural Employment Guarantee Bill 2004 (NREGA) tabled in Parliament on December 21, 2004, was passed on August 23, 2005. The Act seeks to provide guaranteed employment for at least 100 days per year, at the statutory minimum wage, to at least one adult per rural household, who would volunteer to do casual manual labour.[8] One thing is quite clear. Since the bulk of the poor are in the rural sector, the objectives of this act make eminent sense. Such schemes provide a security safety net that is presently not available to the unemployed. Further, if planned imaginatively, such schemes could result in the creation of economic overhead capital: micro watershed development projects are a good example.

Water Resources

Historically, the strategy of treating irrigation as the kingpin of agricultural development has yielded the desired results. Food self-sufficiency was attained through this strategy. For example, today nearly 60 per cent of the crop output is accounted for by irrigated area, which forms about 30 per cent of the cropped area. This also explains why almost 90 per cent of public investment in agriculture was accounted for by irrigation.

In the new millennium, the critical importance of water transcends considerations of merely irrigating land, and agricultural growth will have to be necessarily water-centric.[9] The present government has realised the

---

8. See ch. 8 of this book.
9. Mujumdar, N.A. (2005). "Risk Philosophy: An Enquiry into Risks and Uncertainties" in *Agriculture and the Role of Credit*, NABARD, Mumbai.

critical importance of water: "Water is the lifeline of civilisations. We have been warned that the biggest crisis that the world will face in the 21st century will be crisis of water."[10] The need for integrated water resource management has now become the core of water-policy thinking.

This is in consonance with the trend world over, even between the Second World Water Forum held in 2000 in the Hague and third held in 2003 in Kyoto, ideas had changed. Instead of compartmentalising 'water for health', 'water for food', 'water for environment', a more holistic goal is in sight: 'Water security and sanitation for all, especially for the poor'. One of the 18 targets set under the Millennium Development Goals is: "To halve[11], by 2015, the proportion of people without sustainable access to safe drinking water and basic sanitation." Thus, the United Nations 'Water for Life' decade 2005-2015 was formally launched on March 22, 2005. In fact, as we have already noted, M.S. Swaminathan defines food security as, "Physical, economic, social and ecological access to balanced diet, and clean drinking water for all and forever." Viewed in this broader context, there is a need for a decentralised approach to water harvesting and saving technologies, and equitable water-sharing methodologies based on soil and climatic conditions on the one hand, and sociological factors on the other.

Four interconnected programmes assume significance in this context: watershed development programme, renovation of all water bodies linked to agriculture, which have presently fallen into disuse, correcting the deterioration of public irrigation works, notably state canal systems, due to cumulative neglect of repair and maintenance over the years; and rainwater harvesting. Today, watershed development is seen as the principal strategy for holistic development of rainfed areas, though in the initial stages it was conceived mainly as a measure for moisture conservation and soil stabilisation. The new 'Watershed Plus' approach to watershed development, as spelt out in the Tenth Plan, seeks to ensure convergence of all other programmes that promote economic activities and generate increased employment opportunity. The Union Budget for 2004-2005 proposes a massive scheme to repair, renovate and restore all the water bodies which have fallen into disuse. Finally, rainwater conservation and harvesting has important implications for the groundwater crisis that India is currently facing, due to indiscriminate use of tube-well technology in parts of the country. Equally important is the need to promote micro-

10. Chidambaram, P. (2004). "Budget Speech", July 8.
11. Black, Maggie and Rupert Tolbot (2005). *Water: A Matter of Life and Health*, Oxford University Press, New Delhi, p. 240.

irrigation technology on a large scale through drip and sprinkler irrigation systems.

Diversification of Agriculture

Agricultural development should be considered as an inclusive concept: for instance, animal husbandry, horticulture, dairy development, fisheries, forestry and wildlife, plantations, soil and water conservation, food processing, storage and warehousing, drainage and flood control—all these impinge directly or indirectly, on agricultural development. Diversification of agriculture should be viewed as part of the wider objective of rural diversification.

The livestock sub-sector is particularly important because its development would facilitate many marginal farmers—they form 60 per cent of operational holdings—crossing the threshold of economic viability. Fortunately, since the 1980s, this sub-sector has recorded a much faster growth than the agricultural sector as a whole. The share of the livestock sub-sector in the total value of output of the agriculture sector went on rising consistently to reach 25 per cent in the 1990s. This process of diversification has already been entrenched and likely to gather further momentum[12] because of the more promising prospects of demand for livestock *vis-à-vis* crop products.

Small-scale agro-based industries offer ample scope for moving further in this direction. Historically, developing countries have promoted value added processing of primary products as a path to rural industrialisation. This has important implications for investment in agriculture. The recent committee on capital formation in agriculture has emphasised the need for capital formation for agriculture, in contrast to our conventional approach of capital formation in agriculture. To quote from the committee's report: "As agriculture is getting diversified there is a need to not only augment but also restructure the pattern of investment in agriculture. Historically, the public sector has taken a lead in directing the growth and pattern of investment. We recommend that immediate steps should be taken to improve capital formation for agriculture in both public and private sectors. Otherwise, it may be difficult to sustain agricultural growth and rural purchasing power. Currently, irrigation accounts for the bulk of public investment (above 90 per cent). The new strategy of agricultural

---

12. Sawant, S.D. (1997). "Performance of Indian Agriculture with Special Reference to Regional Variations", *Indian Journal of Agricultural Economics*, July-September.

growth and diversification of agriculture from traditional crop cultivation to horticulture, etc. would require investment in cold storage, rural roads, communication, marketing network and facilities, and warehouses, etc. Simultaneously, efforts should be made to revitalise agriculture through the introduction of biotechnology and other innovations. This would require a substantial increase in investment in research and development for agriculture."[13] Only such a broader approach can facilitate the achievement of the twin objectives of development, namely, accelerating growth of agricultural GDP and promoting equity through reduction in poverty.

Conclusions

This rapid review of the new generation problems faced by Indian agriculture in the new millennium leads us to two important conclusions. First, producing adequate quantum of foodgrains is only a part of the story of self-sufficiency in food. It is also necessary to ensure that the food so produced reaches all the needy. Against this background, exporting foodgrains on a massive scale, we must realise, is a development atrocity. Our focus should, therefore, be henceforth on not merely accelerating agricultural growth but also on empowering more and more poor people with purchasing power to access foodgrains. Employment expansion in the rural sector is thus an ineluctable necessity.

Second, attention of the Indian policymakers should be drawn to the subtle change that seems to have taken place recently in development economics and policy. In the 1990s the market theology of the IMF and World Bank had greatly influenced public policy in many developing countries. The mindless pursuit of market-led growth strategies had diluted the development content of public policy. Indian policymakers of the 1990s were no exception. It had become fashionable to argue that the poor must fend for themselves: food subsidies and input subsidies should be abolished. In fact, it was then argued that the entire mechanism of procurement of foodgrains and the public distribution system (PDS) should be dismantled. The recent UN report on development by Jeffrey D. Sachs provides a welcome correction to this emphasis on market-led growth. By making the millennium development goals (MDGs), the focal point of public policy, the report has succeeded in bringing issues like reduction of poverty, elimination of hunger, promotion of health, and

---

13. Government of India (2003). *Report of the Committee on Capital Formation in Agriculture*, New Delhi, March.

education of the rural poor to the forefront of the development agenda.[14] A direct attack on poverty had become an anathema to policymakers during the market theology phase. It has once again become respectable. Not only government intervention but also a proactive role of government in tackling employment and food security has, thus, been now accepted even by the market theologists.

Reverting to India, the 1990s may have been a lost decade for agriculture but it is heartening to note that the development scenario has changed substantially in the new millennium. It was left to the UPA government to restore the priority of the agricultural sector and of objectives like reduction in poverty and elimination of hunger: its National Common Minimum Programme (NCMP), announced in 2004, reflects this restoration. "Empowering the people, especially the poor, with universal access to education and health, and facilitating their full participation in the growth process through gainful employment will enhance their welfare. It will reinforce the growth process itself. This win-win strategy is the keystone of the economic policy framework of the Government."[15] The target of doubling agricultural credit in the next three years, recognising water resources as a critical factor in accelerating growth and ensuring food security, and the National Rural Employment Guarantee Act, 2005, are concrete instances in point. More recently, an ambitious Bharat Nirman programme has been conceived, under which one crore hectares of un-irrigated land will be irrigated, over 60 lakh rural houses will be built and all villages with a population of 1,000 and above would be connected with roads. Such restoration of priority to agriculture and rural development should go a considerable way towards achieving the objectives of accelerating agricultural growth and reducing poverty.

---

14. *Investing in Development: A Practical Plan to Achieve Millennium Development Goals*, UN, New York, 2005.

15. Chidambaram, P. (2004). "Budget Speech", July 8.

3

The Unaddressed Agenda of Development

There is an euphoria about the current state of the Indian economy, with the Finance Minister waxing eloquent on the robust health of the economy. Such rhapsodies on the so-called 'over-all feel good factor' of the economy are reminiscent of the slogan: "We have never had it so good" of the Margaret Thatcher's Britain. Admittedly, such rhapsodies cannot be dubbed as irrational exuberance because the fundamentals do seem to reflect the buoyancy of the economy. On the external front, the country's foreign exchange reserves touched $ 90 billion by end-October 2003, and are most likely to soar to $ 100 billion by the end of the financial year. Exports continued to be buoyant: during first half of the current financial years, export growth was 10 per cent, close on the heels of a 18 per cent growth recorded during the previous year. Another encouraging feature of the external sector is the emerging current account deficit: the first half of the current financial year recorded a trade deficit of $ 7.1 billion, in contrast to a deficit of $ 3.5 billion recorded in the corresponding period of 2002-03. The current account on balance of payments has been showing surplus for the last couple of years partly because of sluggish growth of non-oil imports. Happily, during the first half of 2003-04, non-oil imports registered a growth of 28 per cent. Growth in capital goods imports is impressive at around 10 to 15 per cent. This signals fresh investment across different industrial sub-sectors. Such current account deficits bolstered by high level of capital goods imports can and do accelerate industrial and overall growth of the economy in the medium-term. The mood regarding foreign direct investment continues to be upbeat. The rupee has been firming up against the US dollar.

On the domestic front, although 2002-03 was a year of severe drought, availability of foodgrains was not affected, thanks to the embarrassingly high level of stocks of foodgrains with the Food Corporation of India (FCI). Foodgrains production dipped to 182.6 million tonnes in 2002-03 and yet foodgrains stocks with FCI continued to remain at a high level of

36.2 million tonnes in February, 2003. Since this year's monsoon was exceptionally good—33 out of 36 meteorological sub-divisions received normal to excess rainfall—*kharif* foodgrains production is estimated to record a rise of 20 per cent over the previous year's crop. Overall foodgrains production may exceed the record level of 212 million tonnes reached in 2001-02. Although at present the level of foodgrains' stocks have been depleted because of large exports, the bumper harvest in the offing may swell the stocks in 2003-04 to the previous record level of 60 to 65 million tonnes. It is these stocks which have helped contain inflation: notwithstanding the severe drought, the underlying inflation rate, represented by the 52 week moving average of the whole-sale price index (WPI) was 3.3 per cent in 2002-03 as compared to the corresponding figure of 3.6 per cent in the preceding year. The forecast of inflation for 2003-04 is 4 or 4.5 per cent. There has been recovery in industrial production during the current year and with the anticipated high growth in agricultural production, national income (GDP) growth may turn out to be around 6.5 to 7.0 per cent. This would be in sharp contrast to a growth of mere 4.4 per cent recorded last year. Given this constellation of macroeconomic indicators, no wonder the Finance Minister is ecstatic about the economy.

Some of us, including some of our policymakers, have not, even now, cast off our colonial baggage of exulting in the commendations of our erstwhile white masters. The recent Report prepared by Goldman Sachs, the well-known Wall Street investment bank, on the growing importance of BRIC countries—Brazil, Russia, India and China—forecasts that India is on its way to becoming the world's third largest economy by 2050. This is supposed to have reinforced the feel good factor.

How far is this ecstasy justified? At the outset, it should be pointed out that the 7 per cent growth forecast for 2003-04 is an aberration rather than part of an abiding trend. In fact GDP growth decelerated from 6.6 per cent in the Eighth Plan (1992-1997) to 5.3 per cent in the Ninth Plan (1997-2002). Even apart from growth trends, I would like to submit that there is a whole bunch of issues on the development agenda, as important as the macroeconomic indicators discussed earlier, which remains unaddressed. This unaddressed agenda includes, elimination of hunger and promotion of social development through the utilisation of the so-called 'surplus' foodgrains, removal of major infrastructural constraints by utilisation of surplus foreign exchange resources, strengthening household sector saving by correction of ill-conceived and distorted interest rate structure, and fiscal policies, and redefining the role of public sector banks and development banks. The most retrogressive mix of policies is the mindless liberalisation of import of gold and equally irresponsible policy of encouraging export of foodgrains on a massive scale. In a country where a sizeable section of the population is, in a manner of speaking in a semi-starvation state are we justified in exporting 10 million tonnes of foodgrains? Are we exporting foodgrains to finance the imports of gold at an obscenely high level of $ 5 billion per year? Are we affluent enough to fritter away our foreign exchange resources for gold consumption rather than utilise them for enhancing growth? Our contemporary policymakers, awed by market theology, are never tired of repeating that food subsidies on the domestic front should be abolished completely. The same experts have no qualms about encouraging the subsidisation of foreign consumers of Indian rice and wheat! Indian exports of rice and wheat are highly subsidised. What a perversion of priorities and travesty of development? These policies are inegalitarian, destructive of savings, and welfare reducing. Correction of these disturbing distortions in development policy also forms part of the Unaddressed Agenda. The crux of the matter is that we must address India-specific situations rather than follow blindly IMF/World Bank theology. We must be intellectually self-confident enough to feel able to attune development policies to India-specific situations. Otherwise there is the danger that we may end up with growth *sans* development.

The most conspicuous evidence of Indian policymakers' dependence on received wisdom and failure to address India-specific issues is the mountain of the so-called 'surplus' foodgrains, the size of which had soared to 64 million tonnes at one point of time. The coexistence of embarrassingly huge stocks of foodgrains with distressingly large unsatisfied demand for foodgrains, reflects the failure of economic reforms; reforms in any meaningful sense, need to be home-grown and not imported from IMF/World Bank manuals. Indian policymakers have not covered themselves in glory in this area.

Of course, the size of the mountain has shrunk to 32 million tonnes now because of the drought and large scale exports in 2002-03. But with the bumper harvest in the offing in 2003-04, the stocks may swell again to 60 million tonnes. Yet precious little has been done to utilise these massive surplus productively. It is not as if the mountain erupted suddenly, taking the policymakers by surprise. Foodgrain stocks with the public sector rose to 29 million tonnes in 1999-2000—well above the buffer stock norm of 21 million tonnes, and have since been rising consistently. India is the abode of the largest number of underfed and undernourished people in the world. According to FAO, more than 225 million Indians remain chronically undernourished: and the UNDP estimates that over half of all Indian pre-schoolers suffer from malnutrition. How did the policymakers respond to this situation? In an over-zealous attempt to cut food subsidies, Government of India has been raising issue prices of foodgrains distributed through the public distribution system (PDS) and consequently, the off-take of foodgrains from the PDS has shown a decline. Foodgrains are, thus, increasingly becoming inaccessible to the poor. This has led to the swelling of stocks with FCI.

Indian policymakers brought up on the diet of the market theology of IMF and World Bank mistake, the minimum support price (MSP) system for rice and wheat, for the bulge in food stocks. These experts fail to recognise that the so-called 'surplus' foodgrains is only an effective demand surplus and not a genuine surplus in the sense of say, wheat surplus in the USA. In fact in the decade of economic reforms, the 1990s, agricultural growth decelerated sharply. The per capita availability of cereals actually declined from 450 grams per day in 1991 to 395 grams in 2001. Even modest projections of demand for cereals in 2020 place the estimate at 260 million tonnes, as compared to the level of 187 million tonnes in 2001. The enormous gap between demand and supply is thus obvious.

Other proponents of the market philosophy make a plea for the abolition of the public distribution system (PDS) itself, to save the Government from the embarrassment of huge stocks. This is like throwing away the baby with the bath water. Public memory is proverbially short, but at least economists should recall that the emergence of PDS itself was is response to the rapacious nature of private trade in foodgrains, under which both farmers and consumers were exploited, through the mechanism of artificially depressing foodgrains prices in the immediate post-harvest period and raising them to unusual heights in the lean season. Whatever may have been the inefficiencies of FCI, it has emerged as an effective counter-veiling force to private trade. In fact, the instruments of MSP, PDS and input subsidy have played a critical role in achieving the twin objectives of accelerated agricultural growth and food security and have conferred benefits on all the sections of the society.

One needs to go further. In this India-specific unique situation, it seems feasible to eliminate hunger first, and poverty later. Analytically, this is an important step towards evolving what might be described as 'the second best' solution. Conventional wisdom stipulates that the problem of poverty can be tackled through higher GDP growth, expansion of employment, and, additional generation of income in secondary occupations and so on. But this process is a long haul and may take at least two decades, as the recent experience of China has demonstrated. We will explain later that even after a decade from now, 130 million people would continue to be below the poverty line. In contrast, this approach of eliminating hunger by using surplus foodgrains meets the test of 'immediacy' because we have the wherewithal to achieve the objective. How does one go about utilising productively the stocks of foodgrains? A number of modalities are available, including linking of rural development works like micro watershed development programmes to utilisation of foodgrains, instituting a "Grain Loans Facility" for all institutions involved in financing rural development programmes like rural cooperatives, RRBs and even NGOs.[1] Also, there is a need to activate the mid-day meal schemes to provide children in government and government assisted primary schools with prepared meals. This scheme confers multiple benefits on the economy. The Centre for Equity Studies (CES), New Delhi, recently surveyed the functioning of the mid-day meal programme in three states, namely, Chhattisgarh, Rajasthan and Karnataka and came to the conclusion: "As things stand mid-day meals programmes have many flaws, but the way to go is forward and not backward. With adequate resources and quality safeguard, mid-day meals can play a major role in improving school attendance, elementary classroom hunger and fostering social equity."[2] In fact universal and nutritious mid-day meals would be a great leap forward towards, the realisation of the right to food. The rate of literacy is only 60 per cent in India, as compared to China's rate of 81 per cent. Similarly, in areas of high incidence of poverty and unemployment, village *panchayats* may be encouraged to run community kitchens. Productive utilisation of the mountain of surplus foodgrains is one of the biggest problems facing the economy today. If there is a separate Ministry to deal with disinvestment, why should there not be a separate Ministry for utilisation of surplus foodgrains? The primordiall objective of eliminating hunger should subsume all other development objectives.

1. "Rural Development: New Perceptions", *Economic and Political Weekly*, Sept. 28, 2002.
2. Drèze, Jean and Aparajita Goyal (2003). "Future of Mid-Day Meals", *Economic and Political Weekly*, November.

Strange are the ways of the Indian policymakers inspired by the market theology. Embarrassed by the mounting stocks of foodgrains—this itself was a result of unimaginative policies—the Government of India began encouraging exports of foodgrains since 2000-01 and during 2001-02, nearly 3 million tonnes of wheat were exported. During the current year, The Economic Survey, 2002-03 states. "This year rice and wheat exports taken together are likely to rise to 10 million tonnes" (page 172). What an amazing perversion of priorities! What is the rationale for promoting foodgrains' exports on such a massive scale when a sizeable proportion of the domestic population is in a state of semi-starvation? It is one thing to promote high value branded commodities like *Basmati* rice exports, but quite another to export ordinary rice and wheat on such a large scale at the cost of domestic consumers. The perversion is compounded by the fact that these exports have a huge subsidy component. Our policymakers who are not tired of repeating that domestic food subsidy should be done away with, do not mind subsidising overseas consumers of India's wheat and rice. The whole range of policy measures, taken to tackle the 'surplus' foodgrains issue clearly shows that the rhetorics of the Tenth Plan on equity and social justice[3] are hollow.

Secondly, the same story of failure to utilise surpluses holds true in respect of the country's foreign exchange reserves which have already soared to $ 90 billion and which are threatening to reach $ 100 billion shortly. What is the response of RBI to this affluence in forex resources? RBI has liberalised foreign exchange allowances for travel, education, medical treatment and so on. Indian corporates and residents can invest abroad and NRIs can repatriate the proceeds of sale of their assets in India. It is as if we are reaching the point of total capital account convertibility. RBI seems to be keen to shed these embarrassingly high level of reserves. The point is that there is an optimum level of forex reserves which the country should sustain to maintain confidence in the economy and currency. It is wasteful to permit accumulation of reserves well beyond this level. For instance, if we assume that the optimum level to be equivalent to the value of say, six months' imports, around $ 30 billion of reserves could be regarded as prudent. Maintaining reserves far in excess of that level is wasteful because the returns on these reserves, invested in developed countries like the US, UK and Germany are the lowest, particularly in the present context when the world is pressing

3. *Tenth Five Year Plan* 2002-07, Vol. I, Box 1.3, p. 9.

through the low interest rate regime. Frittering away these valuable resources through liberalising remittances or outflow generally, as the RBI seems to be doing now, is not the appropriate answer. In fact this approach is reminiscent of the frittering away by India of the huge sterling balances in the Post-War period. Such liberalisation of exchange regulations provide another instance of reforms *sans* development. Instead, one could think in terms of using surplus reserves to remove infrastructure constraints: for instance, power is acting as a major constraint in industrial growth. Why not import some power plants to ease the situation? Constructive use of excess reserves could raise the productive capability of the economy.

Historically, the Planning Commission has been crying hoarse that availability of foodgrains and foreign exchange are acting as a major constraint on growth. When both these constraints are removed finally, why are the contemporary policymakers unable to exploit the situation to accelerate GDP growth and enhance the welfare of the bulk of the population? One begins to wonder whether this is because solutions to these issues do not find a place in the IMF/World Bank theology.

Obviously, our policy response to the emergence of surpluses of foodgrains and forex resources lacks a clear cut strategy and we see a lot of fumbling around.

Let us now turn to the third issue, i.e., savings. In India, unlike developed countries, the main impetus to overall savings comes from the household sector. Small savings form an important component of household sector savings. Financial sector reforms have stunted the growth of small savings, and household savings generally by reducing yields on small savings and bank deposits. As a result of mindless pursuit of low interest rates, perhaps inspired by the corporate lobby, the RBI has landed the banking system in an anarchy of interest rates. Although the prime lending rate is around 10 to 11 per cent, highly rated corporates are able to raise funds from banks at 6 per cent. In sharp contrast, the small farmer was charged, till recently 12 per cent. It was left to the Government of India to lower, since August 2003, the public sector banks' lending rate for agriculture to a ceiling of 9 per cent. The point is that the low interest rate regime was perhaps designed primarily to pamper the private corporate sector, particularly the elite.

As a result of reducing lending rates, banks were compelled to bring down deposit rates which today hover around 5 to 6 per cent. The administered interest rates on small savings, were also reduced.[4] There was yet another blow. The collapse of the Unit Trust of India (UTI) was the mother of all betrayals to the small saver, because both Government of India and RBI were involved in the management of UTI. In terms of fiscal policy, there was discrimination against bank deposits and in favour of equity interest income was and is subject to tax. India is one of the few developing countries that can boast of a high savings rate and these distortions in fiscal and interest rate policies need to be corrected, if the high rate is to be sustained. The Tenth Plan aims to raise gross domestic savings from 23.3 per cent of GDP in the Ninth Plan to 26.8 per cent and this would be feasible, only if, the household sector savings are not discriminated against.

This brings us to the fourth important item on the agenda, namely, financial sector reforms. I have had occasions to demonstrate that the financial sector reforms introduced in the 1990s have, in effect, succeeded in alienating the financial system from the business of development.[5] It is gratifying to note that Tenth Five Year Plan, 2002-07 admits this point: "It is becoming evident, however, that the organised financial sector in India is either unable or unwilling to finance a range of activities that are of crucial importance both for growth and development. Agriculture, unorganised manufacturing, and services and various types of infrastructure are instances of such sectors. The recent financial sector reforms have naturally focussed primarily on improving the viability and stability of financial institutions, without adequately addressing this issue. It is, therefore, necessary to consider methods of encouraging the financial sector to finance such activities without impinging on its viability or compromising on prudential concerns" (Vol. I, page 13, para 1-52). Elsewhere, I have analysed this issue in-depth and have shown clearly that it was not inability in the sense of inadequate resource availability, but unwillingness that was responsible for the emergence of such a situation.[6] During this phase of reforms, the banking system was highly liquid, with the credit-deposit ratio hovering around 50 per cent. The Tenth Plan also admits that in the euphoria of economic reforms, agriculture was neglected. This is reflected in the deceleration of public investment in agriculture and also of flow of credit to the sector. No wonder agricultural

4. "Small Savings and Market Mythology", *Economic and Political Weekly*, January 29, 2002.

5. Mujumdar, N.A. (2002). *Financial Sector Reforms and India's Economic Development*, Academic Foundation, New Delhi.

6. Ibid.

growth fell sharply from 4.69 per cent per year in the Eighth Plan (1992-1997) to 2.06 per cent in the Ninth Plan (1997-2002). The Tenth Plan makes the appropriate noises: "Agricultural development must be viewed as a core element of the plan, since growth in this sector is likely to lead to the widest spread of benefits especially to the rural poor. The first generation of reforms concentrated on the industrial economy and reforms in the agricultural sector were neglected. This must, change in the Tenth Plan" (Vol. I, page 9). PSBs, which have failed even today to meet the credit target of 18 per cent of net bank credit to agriculture—the actual level was some 15 per cent in 2002-03—should enhance their presence in the rural sector with a view to facilitating higher of agricultural growth, of the non-farm sector, and generally decentralised development.

PSBs must absolve themselves of the new banking culture, patterned on the American banking paradigm which has led to the focus on the three "Cs"—Corporate elite, Capital market-related activities, and Consumer credit. The economic reforms seem to have been aimed at pampering the corporate elite: artificial props to develop the capital market goaded PSBs to involve themselves increasingly in the capital market and related activities, facilitating external commercial borrowings, low interest rate regime and so on. As the Tenth Plan has rediscovered, the solutions to large scale unemployment, poverty and hunger, cannot be sought in the development of large and medium industries alone. Hence, we need a Mahatma Gandhi in the financial sector to redirect financial flows, both investment and working capital, to the resurrection of agriculture, and a whole range of activities relating to decentralised development. Employment, particularly rural employment, has received a setback during the reform era. During the 1980s and the early part of 1990s, the average growth rate of employment was 2 per cent per annum: this rate dropped to 1.1 per cent in the later part of the 1990s. Since employment holds the key to tackle poverty and hunger, employment intensive growth should be our objective in the coming years. The current backlog of unemployment of around 9 per cent equivalent to 35 million persons is alarmingly high. It is in this context that the Prime Minister's vision of creation of 100 million jobs over the next 10 years is taken as the basis for targeting the creation of 50 million employment opportunities during the Tenth Plan. Even if this target is achieved, the unemployment rate would remain at 5 per cent. In terms of absolute numbers this is quite high. Similarly, reduction in poverty through GDP growth is also going to be a long haul. The mandated reduction in poverty rate of 5 percentage points during the Tenth Plan and another 10 percentage points during the Eleventh Plan, will still leave more than 11 per cent of the population or about 130 million people below the poverty line in 2012. It is as if the policymakers are throwing up their hands saying that the situation is hopeless. Do the policymakers expect the "semi-starving India", if I might use the term, to always remain with us?

Again, inspired by the IMF World Bank theology, Indian policymakers have begun to de-emphasise development banks and attempt to develop the capital market. In the process they have decimated, by misconceived policies, the Industrial Development Bank of India (IDBI) which has had an excellent track record. There was a time when many countries used to send their experts to study the IDBI profile so that it can be replicated in their own countries. Thanks to economic reforms, IDBI is in a moribund state today. It is gratifying to note that the Parliamentary Committee has stipulated that in its new *avatar*—converted into a bank—it should retain its development character. With all the rhetoric and the various artificial props given to boost the capital market—like throwing open portfolio investment to Foreign Institutional Investors (FIIs), prodding public sector banks (PSBs) to involve themselves increasingly, both directly and indirectly, in the equity market and fiscal concessions—these efforts have been a heroic failure. The annual average level of new capital raised during the recent few years was only Rs. 5,000 crore, as against Rs. 10,000 crore during early 1990s. In fact, the expectation then was that the capital raised through new issues would soar to Rs. 50,000 crores per year towards the end of the 1990s. The simultaneous growth of the private placement segment to enormous dimensions—it is able to raise some Rs. 60,000 crores per year—is itself an indictment of policy package designed to boost the capital market. Not withstanding the sound and fury made presently of Sensex reaching the 5,000 level, in terms of mobilisation of resources for the corporate sector, capital market provides a case study of aborted growth. Even PSBs which have been highly liquid—the credit-deposit ratio has been hovering around 50 to 52 per cent—should be encouraged to extend medium-term credit to industries. Perhaps the wise policy would have been to encourage both development banks and the capital market to finance industrial growth.

Employment holds the key to eradication of poverty but the expansion in employment will not be generated by large and medium industries. One has to look for decentralised growth of a multitude of tiny and small industries in the rural and semi-urban sectors. The Chinese experience is illuminating in this context. To facilitate such broad-based growth we have to develop SHGs, micro-credit institutions, and increasingly seek to involve NGOs in the process. It is encouraging that RBI has begun to take, recently, some initiatives in this direction.

Finally, the most retrogressive reform is the liberalisation of the import of gold. The annual average level of imports of gold works out to a staggering figure of $ 5 billion, or nearly Rs. 25,000 crore. Did we raise $ 5.5 billion of forex resources through Resurgent India Bonds (RIBs) to finance the import of gold? Did we export 10 million tonnes of foodgrains to finance the import of gold? Import of gold is inegalitarian and destructive of savings because financial savings which could have been channeled to productive purposes, would be diverted to the unproductive investment in gold. Today, in metropolitan and bigger towns there are more jewellery shops than grocery shops. Surely, the WTO did not prescribe the liberalisation of gold imports and this is liberalisation with a vergence. This is a clear case of perversion of priorities in economic reforms, or the ugly face of reforms, a face that has nothing to do even remotely with development.

Summing up, the main theme that I have sought to develop in this lecture is that the current euphoria about the 'overall feel-good factor' should not lull our policymakers into a sense of complacency. The buoyancy of the economy is in a sense ephemeral: this not only needs to be sustained but also be converted into a broad-based growth. It is here that the Unaddressed Agenda becomes of immediate relevance. The Tenth Plan does make appropriate noises: "It is important to re-emphasise that the equity related objectives of the Plan, which are extremely important, are intimately linked to the growth objective, and the attainment of one may not be possible without the attainment of the other. For example, high rates of growth are essential if we want to ensure sufficient expansion of sustainable gainful employment opportunities for our expanding labour force, and a sufficient increase in the incomes of the poor and the disadvantaged... It is also true that high growth rates may not be sustainable if they are not accompanied by a dispersion of purchasing power which can provide the demand needed to support the increase in output..." (Tenth Plan, Vol. I, page 9). The tragedy is that the Tenth Plan merely makes appropriate noises without providing a concrete blue-print for translating these ideas into reality. Nor does the Tenth Plan make any effort to explore the ways of exploiting fully the benefits of our surplus foodgrains and forex resources. The Plan again maintains a studied silence on the anti-development policies of exporting foodgrains and importing gold. It is, therefore, imperative that the Unaddressed Agenda is appropriately incorporated into the core development agenda: perhaps that is the only way by which growth with development can be ensured.

4

Redefining the Approach to Poverty Reduction and Development

India has been in the business of poverty reduction for more than 50 years, since the inception of planning in 1950-51. And yet more than a quarter of the total population continues to live below the poverty line even today. If China could reduce the magnitude of its poverty to a mere 3 per cent of the population in a span of two decades, what went wrong with India? Even assuming that the Indian economy would manage to remain in high growth trajectory of 8 per cent of GDP growth in the coming years, it would take perhaps another two decades to eliminate poverty. We have lived with the wretchedness of absolute shortage of foodgrains supplies in the 1960s, when the average annual imports of wheat hovered around 3 million tonnes. We survived through the munificence of America which supplied wheat to India under its PL 480 programme. In sharp contrast, India today has emerged, as contemporary policymakers would have us believe, as a major exporter of rice and wheat in the world market; India's exports of rice and wheat aggregated to staggering figure of more than 10 million tonnes in 2003-04. The coexistence of alarmingly large unsatisfied domestic demand for foodgrains with massive exports of foodgrains is a clear reflection of our muddle-headed food management policy formulated on the basis of market theology: abolish subsidies for domestic consumption of foodgrains but encourage subsidisation of foodgrains exports. It is this mess of food management policy which warrants redefinition of our basic approach to poverty reduction. Eliminate hunger first and poverty later. For this rather unconventional approach, which is appropriate for the present India-specific situation, to succeed, three ingredients of development policy mix are essential: decentralised and broad-based growth, good governance and concern for social safety net. The package of programmes to be undertaken under such an approach can be so designed that many programmes become economically viable and the package, taken as a whole, can be rendered fiscally sustainable.

Poverty and Foodgrains Exports

The Tenth Five Year Plan begins the discussion on poverty alleviation in the following words:

"At the beginning of the new millennium, 260 million people in the country did not have incomes to access a consumption basket which defines the poverty line. Of these, 75 per cent were in the rural areas. India is home to 22 per cent of the world's poor. Such a high incidence of poverty is a matter of concern in view of the fact that poverty eradication has been one of the major objectives of the development planning process. Indeed, poverty is a global issue. Its eradication is considered integral to humanity's quest for sustainable development. Reduction of poverty in India, is, therefore vital for the attainment of international goals."[1]

Or, take the Budget speech of the Finance Minister, who while presenting the Interim Budget on February 3, 2004, stated:

"We believe, Sir, that both are necessary: a vision for a resurgent India and, simultaneously an awakening so that the disadvantaged of our land are lifted beyond poverty. We hold that economic development is not about economics alone, it is always, simultaneously, a political statement too, for 'development' devoid of compassion is a misnomer. Of course, growth statistics are very important, they are vital inputs; but they must also be the indices that assist us in designing distributive justice. It is for that reason that 'gross national contentment' is so important, as the catalyst that motivates redoubled national endeavour. It is from seeking national contentment that objectives are born: *Garib ke pet me dana, Garibini ki kutia main anna.*"[2]

Nobel sentiments indeed. But look at the situation at the ground level. India's exports of rice and wheat are estimated to have reached or even exceeded 10 million tonnes in 2003-04. Shri Sharad Yadav, Minister for Consumer Affairs, Food and Public Distribution[3] exults in this achievement. "Today, India has emerged as the World's third largest exporter of rice and the seventh largest exporter of wheat. The country has earned foreign exchange of $ 4 billion through these exports. Though maintaining domestic food security will continue to be top priority, the country's newly acquired position as a major exporter of foodgrains will

1. Planning Commission, *Tenth Five Year Plan*, 2002-2007, New Delhi, Vol. II, p. 293.
2. Singh, J. (2004). "Budget Speech of Finance Minister", February 3.
3. Government of India, *Economic Survey*, 2002-03, p. 172.

be protected."[4] In a similar vein, Food Corporation of India (FCI) in a recent advertisement proclaims: "Congratulations to our farmers who have created surplus stock of foodgrains, ensuring no death from hunger."[5]

Concern for good governance and for social safety net must form important ingredients of any meaningful development plan. Unfortunately, contemporary policymakers in India seem to be unwilling to look into subtleties of development beyond the IMF/World Bank models built on market theology. In fact such concerns for the poor, as illustrated above, are being used to merely window-dress growth strategies drawn up on the basis of market theology.

Is there, a surplus of foodgrains in today's India? India continues to be the abode of 260 million people who are in a state of chronic semi-starvation, as admitted by the Planning Commission. In addition, UNDP estimates that over one-half of all Indian pre-schoolers suffer from malnutrition. Against this background, how does one justify the export of foodgrains on a massive scale as in 2003-04? Neither the scholarly document of the Tenth Plan nor the Budget Speech even attempt to provide the rationale for such massive exports. Export of small quantities of high value branded foodgrains like the Basmati rice is indeed understandable. Do we need the foreign exchange so badly that we are compelled to export foodgrains at the cost of domestic food security? Not at all. Our foreign exchange reserves have soared to an unprecedented level of more than $ 100 billion and the RBI is trying to reduce this embarrassingly high level by liberalising the outflow of foreign exchange with reckless abandon. In fact what did we do with $ 4 billion of foreign exchange earned by foodgrains exports? We imported gold: the average annual imports of gold were around $ 5 billion during the last three or four years. It is as if the contemporary policymakers are asking the people: never mind if you cannot afford to buy foodgrains, deck yourself with gold ornaments and be happy!

Market theology has messed up the situation and led to the formation of the muddle-headed food policy. In the first place, market theologists were keen on abolishing domestic food subsidies. This resulted in raising the issue prices of foodgrains distributed through the public distribution system (PDS) successively. The net result was that the off-take of foodgrains from the public distribution system declined substantially over the more recent years, thereby, swelling the stocks with the Food

4. For excertps from the Interview with the Minister, *Swagat* Magazine, December 2003.

5. *The Times of India*, January 28, 2004.

Corporation of India (FCI). In other words, foodgrains became increasingly inaccessible to the poorer sections of the population. These stocks soared to more than 60 million tonnes at one point of time. Embarrassed by such huge stocks co-existing with large unsatisfied domestic demand for foodgrains, the government sought an easy way out: exports of foodgrains. What is worse, our exports of foodgrains are highly subsidised. For instance, during the four years 2000-01 to 2003-04, the price realised on rice exports by FCI has been generally lower than the issue price of rice through the PDS (Appendix A-4.1). In other words, the issue price of grains for exports was highly subsidised. The same market theologists, who are crying hoarse against domestic food subsidies are encouraging the subsidising of foreign consumers of Indian foodgrains! This is a concrete proof that the refrain of the Tenth Plan that we are pursuing growth with equity, or of the budget speech that we are aiming at development with compassion, are no more than rhetoric.

Redefining the Basic Approach

The need to redefine our basic approach to poverty reduction stems from the following three factors. First, conventional wisdom stipulates that the problem of poverty can be tackled through higher GDP growth, expansion of employment, and generation of supplementary income through subsidiary occupations and so on. But the process is a long haul and may take at least two decades. This is the conclusion one can derive from the analysis of trends in poverty as provided in the Tenth Plan. The mandated reduction in poverty rate of 5 per cent point during the Tenth Plan and another 10 per cent point reduction during Eleventh Plan will still leave more than 11 per cent of the population or about 130 million people below the poverty line in 2012. This is predicated on the assumption that high GDP growth of 8 per cent would be sustained throughout the period. To eliminate poverty totally or nearly totally may take another decade. It is as if the policymakers are throwing up their hands, declaring that the situation is hopeless. Do the contemporary policymakers expect the 'semi-starving India' to remain with us always?

Second, the co-existence of embarrassingly large stock of foodgrains with FCI with alarmingly high level of unsatisfied domestic demand for foodgrains is an anachronism. The so-called 'surplus' foodgrains, on the basis of which contemporary policymakers seem to build their strategy for growth is only an 'effective demand surplus' and not a genuine surplus. If domestic food security is to be ensured, the so-called surplus evaporates. In any other country such massive exports of foodgrains against the background of underfed and undernourished population of a sizeable proportion would have exploded into a revolution. But ours is an ancient civilisation known for its quiescence. The tragedy of Indian planning is that over the years, we have developed the technology and the institutional framework to produce adequate quantities of foodgrains, or cereals at any rate: but we simply do not know how to take these foodgrains to the needy. The muddle-headedness of food management policy discussed earlier reflects this tragedy. Food security in a meaningful sense, is enured not by merely producing an adequate quantum of foodgrains but also by reaching of these grains to the needy. In fact, the issue is so important that the Tenth Plan should have devoted a whole chapter to find an appropriate solution to the problem of food delivery mechanism which would ensure food security. In any case, we must redefine our basic approach to poverty reduction by stipulating: eliminate hunger first, and poverty later. This redefined approach meets the test of 'immediacy' because we do not have to wait for two decades to achieve the objective. Fortunately, we have the wherewithal to eliminate hunger, here and now.

The third factor relates to the *modus operandi* of reaching food to the needy. FAO defines food security as: "The physical, economic access for all people, at all times enough food for an active, healthy life, with the non-risk of losing such access and as such is directly connected with livelihood in developing countries." The task of providing access to food is thus inextricably interwoven with the livelihood or employment, because a majority of the poor are not only asset-less but also without any assured or continuous employment. This brings us to the employment situation. The current backlog of unemployment is around 9 per cent or equivalent to 35 million persons and this is far too high. On the basis of the Prime Minister's vision of creating 100 million employment opportunities over the next 10 years, the Tenth Plan has set a target of creation of 50 million jobs during the next five years. If this target is achieved, unemployment is likely to decline to some 5 per cent by the end of the Tenth Plan. To be able to realise this target, the focus will have to be on a wide range of sectors such as agriculture and allied sectors, construction, tourism, transport and small scale industries (SSIs), micro-enterprises, retail trade and so on. The organised sector can do precious little to meet the enormous employment demand and thus the focus would have to be on decentralised and broad-based growth.

The redefined approach to poverty reduction could be summed up as following: even assuming that the Indian economy continues to remain in a high growth trajectory of 8 to 10 per cent GDP growth in the next decade, reduction of poverty to an acceptable level will take a long time. We cannot afford to live with a semi-starving population of an alarming magnitude for long, especially when we have been able to produce adequate or nearly adequate quantity of foodgrains. Elimination of hunger in the immediate run by utilisation of all the quantities of foodgrains we produce—making allowance for buffer stocks—should therefore be accepted as the 'second best' solution in the given configuration of circumstances. Contemporary policymakers must realise that, there are no 'exportable surpluses' of foodgrains; they should also grow out of their received wisdom of market theology and begin to design an appropriate foodgrains delivery mechanism to reach foodgrains to the needy. This mechanism would be consistent with broad-based and decentralised growth and in fact, the two could be made mutually reinforcing. The constellation of this mechanism and other supportive policies could be rendered fiscally viable, making some allowance also for an element of social safety net.

Decentralised Growth

Employment expansion is the ideal way by which the poor would be empowered to have access to foodgrains. Food for Work Programme lends itself admirably to serve the purpose. In fact there is no reason why the National Highways Development Project which includes the Golden Quadrilateral connecting the four metro cities of Delhi, Mumbai, Chennai and Kolkata, could not have been converted into one of such programmes. At least part of the wages of the labour employed on the project could have been paid in kind, that is, in foodgrains. This needs to be supplemented by other modalities such as linking rural development works like micro watershed development programmes to utilisation of foodgrains, instituting 'Grain Loans Facility' for all institutions involved in rural development programmes like rural cooperatives, RRBs and NGOs. I have spelt out the possibilities elsewhere.[6] As already discussed in ch. 3 there is enormous scope for enlarging the coverage of the mid-day meals scheme, to provide children in government and government assisted primary schools with prepared meals.

6. "Rural Development: New Perceptions", *Economic and Political Weekly*, September 28, 2002.

The Tenth Plan document itself provides a number of concrete programmes which would generate sizeable rural employment. The new 'watershed plus' approach to watershed development seeks to ensure convergence of all other programmes that promote economic activities and generate increased employment opportunities. Conscious efforts to promote non-farm employment and increased land access for the landless as well as promotion of SHGs form part of the new approach. Then again, the utilisation of wastelands. Out of the estimated area of 107 million hectares of degraded land, 64 million hectares are categorised as wastelands. Under this programme, all such lands under the control of government or *Panchayats* would be parcelled out in viable units and allotted to landless scheduled caste and tribe farmers, small and marginal farmers, and educated rural youth, for cultivation. Besides the wastelands, some of the areas under reserved forests are also unutilised or under-utilised. It is envisaged that local community access would be provided to grass and fodder from the forest area and the community would be encouraged to produce grasses and fodder and the medicinal and aromatic plants in the under-utilised areas under forest cover. Rainwater conservation and harvesting hold the key to sustainable development of rainfed areas. Hence, there is a need to move way from the conventional soil conservation approach of safe disposal of run-off water to rainwater harvesting and conservation. Then there is organic farming, with organic seed and compost preparation.

The point is that there are a thousand ways by which rural employment could be generated and any particular programme chosen needs to be area-specific. In the final analysis, productive utilisation of all foodgrains domestically—and not through exports—should be the overriding objective of development policy.

To what extent these and related schemes would be economically viable and fiscally sustainable? Obviously, many of the schemes discussed earlier would create economic and social over-head capital. Use of foodgrains through mid-day meals is tantamount to investment in education. In fact, we should not feel shy of devising some schemes like community kitchens for the old and the destitutes in the villages. India cannot afford, as yet, to institute a comprehensive social security scheme on the lines of those provided in developed countries like the UK or USA. Through the various modalities discussed earlier and with appropriate supportive policies in place, India can at least seek to guarantee the right to food to all its citizens. If necessary, an 'employment cess' can be levied on all those employed to guarantee resources to support the network of programmes outlined above. Taking the package as a whole, it seems feasible to render it fiscally sustainable.

Governance in Rural Administration

Good governance in rural administration, as also in the management of rural financial institutions is a crucial determinant of the success of rural development programmes. Three concrete cases can be cited to demonstrate how lack of or bad governance frustrates the successful implementation of rural development programmes. First, take the case of the Food-for-Work Programme, which was started in 2000-01 as a component of the Employment Assurance Scheme (EAS) in eight notified drought affected States of Chhattisgarh, Gujarat, Himachal Pradesh, Madhya Pradesh, Orissa, Rajasthan, Maharashtra and Uttaranchal. The Programme aims at augmenting food security through wage employment. Foodgrains were supplied to States free of cost. Unfortunately, the record of the lifting of foodgrains allotted for the scheme from the Food Corporation of India (FCI) has been very disappointing. For instance, against an allocation of 35.31 lakh tonnes of foodgrains, only 21.26 lakh tonnes were lifted by the target states up to January 2002. Was the Centre not persuasive enough? Or, do the States need to be sensitised[7] about the misery of poverty, unemployment and the state of semi-starvation? In all the target states, there is enormous scope for launching schemes to utilise foodgrains provided by the Centre at zero cost.

Second, take the case of utilisation of funds, under Rural Infrastructure Development Fund (RIDF). This fund was originally set up with NABARD in 1995-96 with a corpus of Rs. 2,000 crore with the major objective of providing funds to state governments to enable them to complete ongoing infrastructure projects pertaining to irrigation, flood protection, rural roads and bridges. The scope of RIDF has been progressively widened to include lending to *Gram Panchayats*, self-help groups for implementing village level infrastructure projects. Although the total corpus adds up to Rs. 34,000 crore as of 2002-03, the overall utlisation of these funds by the states has been dismal at only 58 per cent. In fact the percentage of[8] utilisation declined to 40 and 18 in 2002 and 2003. Are the reconnaissance efforts of NABARD to identify eligible projects unsatisfactory? Or, are the States indifferent to rural development? One begins to wonder.

7. Government of India, *Tenth Five Year Plan, 2002-07*, Vol. I, p. 297.

8. Reserve Bank of India (2003). *Report on Trend and Progress of Banking in India, 2002-03*, p. 103.

The third case relates to the financial institutions. As I have demonstrated elsewhere the financial sector reforms introduced in the 1990s have, in effect, succeeded in alienating the financial system from the business of development.[9] Admitting this conclusion, the Tenth Plan states: "It is being evident, however, that the organised financial sector in India is either unable or unwilling to finance a range of activities that are of crucial importance both for growth and development. Agriculture, unorganised manufacturing and services and various types of infrastructure are instances of such sectors. The recent financial sector reforms have naturally focussed primarily in improving viability and stability of financial institutions, without adequately addressing this issue. It is therefore necessary to consider methods of encouraging the financial sector to finance such activities, without impinging on its viability or compromising on prudential concerns."[10] Public sector banks which have historically played a pioneering role in reaching out to farmers in the post-nationalisation period, have failed even today to meet the credit target of 18 per cent of net bank credit to agriculture: the actual level was some 15 per cent in 2002-03. This is not because of their inability, since banks have remained highly liquid during the recent years with credit-deposit ratio hovering around 50 per cent. It is high time that public sector banks and financial institutions changed their post-reform attitude to agricultural and rural development.

Overall, the picture that emerges is clear. Agricultural growth or rural development in general is not constrained by lack of resources, both financial and in terms of wage-goods. It is lack of governance which is hampering growth. Fuller utilisation of these resources would go a long way towards facilitating higher growth and eliminating hunger. And good governance is a prerequisite for fuller utilisation.

Conclusion

Without waiting for two decades or so to eliminate poverty through the conventional route, it makes sense to redefine our immediate development objective in terms of eliminating hunger here and now, by utilising what contemporary Indian policymakers consider as 'surplus foodgrains'. Let our policymakers disabuse their mind of the idea of 'surplus' and seek to match the so-called surplus with large unsatisfied

9. For detailed discussion: Mujumdar, N.A. (2002). *Financial Sector Reforms and India's Economic Development*, Academic Foundation, New Delhi.

10. *Tenth Plan*, Vol. I, p. 13, para 1.52.

demand for foodgrains. To be able to achieve this objective in the short-run, decentralised and broad-based growth of the economy needs to be promoted. Although the Tenth Plan attempts to sketch the broad contours of such growth, it does not provide a blueprint of the institutional framework which can translate such growth into reality. Microcredit institutions, micro-enterprises, self-help groups (SHGs) and NGOs and the private sector on the one hand; establishing and strengthening links and cooperation between, government, panchayati raj institutions, NGOs and the private sector on the other hand. Such networking needs to be institutionalised taking into account the state-specific circumstances. Such institutionalisation also can facilitate decentralised and broad-based growth.

Appendix A-4.1

Prices of Rice Sold by Food Corporation of India (FCI)

(Rs. per Quintal)

Year	*For Export*	*Issue Prices for BPL Families*	*Issue Prices for APL Families*
2000-01	420	565	830
2001-02	495	565	830
2002-03	551	565	730
2003-04	581	565	850

Notes : BPL - Below Poverty Line.
APL - Above Poverty Line.

Source : These data, published in *The Economic Times* on 2-1-2004, are based on an answer provided by the Minister of State for Consumer Affairs, Food and Public Distribution to a question in Rajya Sabha.

5

First Principles of Foodgrains Management

The recent announcement that Government of India would import a massive quantity of 5 to 6 million tonnes of wheat this year, has come as a shock for two reasons. First, what about the oft-repeated statements of both policymakers and professional economists that India has become self-sufficient in rice and wheat, and in fact has generated some 'exportable surpluses' in some years? Second, such massive imports are perfectly understandable in years of drought or near-drought situations. But the year 2005-06 was a fairly good agricultural year: the first advanced estimates of foodgrains production for 2005-06, released by the Ministry of Agriculture in September 2005 placed *kharif* foodgrains output at 105 million tonnes, that is about 2 million tonnes higher than that of the previous year. Production of *rabi* foodgrains was expected to be around at last years' level of 101 million tonnes, with wheat production expected to be at last years' level of 72 million tonnes. In fact, some agricultural scientists had forecast wheat production at 73 million tonnes. What then is the provocation for such massive imports of wheat?

The ostensible reason is that central foodgrains stocks fell below the buffer stock norms: for instance, in October 2005, wheat stocks fell short of the norm marginally by 0.7 million tonnes. But the *Economic Survey*, 2005-06 is far from apologetic about the shortfall: "However, the present shortfall in the stocks over the buffer norms is not considered alarming and appears sufficient to meet the requirements under Targeted Public Distribution System (TPDS), welfare schemes, and open market sales during the current financial year. The shortfall is expected to lead to a reduction in carrying costs and the subsidies bill of the Government" (p. 95). Between end-February 2006 when the *Economic Survey* was released and May 2006, why has the perception of the Government of India changed so drastically? Of course, procurement of wheat during the current season so far has been much lower than the level last year. But does it warrant such panic reaction?

This note seeks to argue that this episode of importing wheat on such a large scale should not be viewed in isolation but as a part the muddle-headed policy of foodgrains management pursued during the 1990s and the five or six years of the new millennium. These were the years of economic reforms and liberalisation of the Indian economy and the majority of the Indian policymakers during this period were intoxicated with the market theology of the IMF and the World Bank.

Reduction of the Centre's Budget deficit was regarded as the *summum bonum* of macroeconomic management and the axe fell heavily on food subsidies. The net result has been the alienation of poorer sections of the population from the public distribution system (PDS)—a system that was specifically designed for them originally. The size of subsidies was sought to be reduced by what one might call "economics of exclusion": by reducing the number of families eligible for accessing PDS and by raising the issue prices of foodgrains as a result of which foodgrains became increasingly inaccessible to the poor sections. The current episode of importing wheat, forms part of this tragic tale which needs to be told more in sorrow than in anger. This track record of inept management of foodgrains also warrants that we enunciate the first principles of foodgrains management in a poor economy.

Ironically, a couple of years ago, we paraded ourselves as exporters of foodgrains. Indian exports of rice and wheat during the three consecutive years 2001-02 to 2003-04 soared to more than 27 million tonnes: 46 lakh tonnes in 2001-02, 125 lakh tonnes in 2002-03 and 103 lakh tonnes in 2003-04. The official document of the Government of India, *Economic Survey*, 2003-04, exulted in this achievement. "The exports of foodgrains (rice and wheat) have picked up considerably in recent years accounting for around 20 per cent of agricultural exports. The government's special efforts to encourage exports of foodgrains in recent years, through grant of World Trade Organization (WTO), compatible subsidies has placed India as one of the leading exporters of foodgrains in the international market." (p. 106) Little did the authors of the Economic Survey realise that in the next couple of years India would end up as the largest importer of wheat in the world.

Indian policymakers appear to have become cortically blind during this phase in the sense that their eyes could see but their brains could not register the image of what they saw. Otherwise, how could they ignore the fact that India is the abode of the largest number of underfed and chronically undernourished persons in the world? According to FAO, 852 million persons in the world are underfed and undernourished, and India accounts for some 225 to 250 million persons falling in this category. A recent World Bank study estimates that about 47 per cent of children below 3 years in India are undernourished. Persisting malnutrition has a severally debilitating effect on human development and this has serious implications for economic growth in general.

The apparent rationale for foodgrains exports on such a massive scale, as mentioned above, was that foodgrains stocks with the centre reached embarrassingly high levels, well beyond the stipulated buffer norms. For instance, at one point of time, stocks soared to 60 million tonnes. The argument was that such stocks would greatly increase carrying costs and thereby, inflate foodgrains subsidy requirements. But the most pertinent question to pose is: why were stocks allowed to rise to such unprecedented levels? It is here that the tragic story unfolds itself. Of course, there is the basic problem of 'effective demand surplus' of foodgrains: because the poor do not have income, or purchasing power, foodgrains remain unsold and hence the apparent, not real, 'surplus'. What is worse, on this surplus, was superimposed what can be called as 'forced savings of foodgrains', on the analogy of the erstwhile Soviet Union's concept of forced savings. There were two policy initiatives, both highly regressive, taken during this phase, which resulted in bolstering foodgrains stocks with the Centre. Dr. Abhijit Sen's highly analytical Report on 'Long Term Grain Policy' provides interesting insights into this intriguing situation.[1] This Report has not received the attention it deserves during current discussions on foodgrains management, perhaps because Dr. Sen, the Chairman of the Committee, refused to join the chorus of market theology.

First, the Government introduced in 1997, targeting in the PDS in the form of Targeted PDS or TPDS. "Thus, the narrow targeting of the PDS based on absolute income poverty is likely to have excluded a large part of the nutritionally vulnerable population from the PDS" (p. 59). The introduction of the TPDS, followed by the virtual exclusion of the Above Poverty Line (APL) population due to the new price regime led to a sharp decline in the off-take of foodgrains from PDS. In 1991, 20.8 million tonnes of rice and wheat were distributed through PDS network. In the first few years of the introduction of economic reforms, the quantities

1. Sen, Abhijit (2002). *Report of the High Level Committee on Long Term Grain Policy for the Country,* Ministry of Consumer Affairs, Food and Public Distribution, Government of India, July, New Delhi.

distributed declined, reaching 14 million tonnes in 1994. The introduction of targeted PDS, referred to above, led to further declines: the off-takes in 2000-01 and 2001-02 were 11.7 million tonnes and 13.8 million tonnes (p. 63). Thus, it is clear that the soaring of stocks with the Centre, which provided the excuse for exports, was a direct result of this policy initiative of 'exclusion'. The second dimension of 'exclusion' relates to prices of cereals. Cereal prices in real terms rose sharply during the 1990s reversing the earlier trend. The Sen Committee provides concrete data on price rise. On Wholesale Price Index (WPI) basis, real cereals prices increased by 33.2 per cent between 1990-91 and 1999-2000 (p. 44). This trend exposes the absence of policy initiatives to moderate the rise in prices of cereals. Especially when foodgrains stocks with the Centre were so high, it should have been possible to moderate the price rise by appropriate market intervention by the Food Corporation of India (FCI). We should cease to treat the FCI as a glorified godown keeper but use it as an effective mechanism to moderate the prices of rice and wheat, even in the open market. Such high price rise in cereals meant that rice and wheat became increasingly inaccessible to the poorer sections of the population.

Both these policy initiatives of 'exclusion', namely cutting down the number of persons who have access to concessionally priced foodgrains under PDS, and raising the prices of cereals were obviously inspired by the policymakers' obsession with cutting down the Centre's budgetary deficit by reducing the quantum of food subsidy. In a way, reduction in the Centre's budget deficit can be regarded as an intermediate target, the final target being development. Unfortunately, Indian policymakers, blinded by market theology, sacrified the final target in order to achieve the intermediate target. In the process, Indian policymakers lost sight of the broader objectives of development, namely, reduction in poverty or hunger. Exports of foodgrains of staggering dimensions mentioned above, in the Indian context, can only be regarded as development atrocity, as I have discussed elsewhere.[2] Policymakers abrogated the first principles of foodgrains management in a poor economy.

The Sen Committee seeks to drive home this point in the following words:

> We call upon government not to view these stocks as a burden which when reduced, will reduce the fiscal deficit. We believe that the present juncture is one where the nation should commit itself to eradication of

2. See ch. 2 of this book.

> destitution and chronic malnutrition and rethink many aspects of food policy...Nonetheless, the poor still spend about a third of their budget on cereals and derive almost three-fourths of their nutrition from this. About three-quarters of cereals consumption is in rural areas and grain policy will be critical as rural India diversifies its income, and regions specialise (p. 5).

The first principles of foodgrains management in India which has a sizeable population of the poor are now clear that the bulk of the foodgrains produced in the country should be utilised for domestic consumption, apart from maintaining buffer stocks. Of course, export of high value foodgrains like *Basmati* rice would continue but the quantities involved would be marginal. This should be treated as a primordial priority superseding all other considerations. Both pricing of cereals in the PDS and conditionalities of access to PDS should be so designed as to promote maximum utilisation of available cereals. Although we have many other schemes of foodgrains utilisation like *Antyodaya* and other welfare schemes, these have come to be regarded as no more than tokenism. This is reflected in the poor off-take of foodgrains under these schemes: for instance, in 2004-05 *Antyodaya* scheme accounted for only half-a-million tonnes and the welfare schemes for about one million tonnes. The most conspicuous example of the indifference of State Governments is the Food-for-Work Programme. Although the centre provides foodgrains free of cost to states for this purpose, states do not utilise the full quota of their allotment. In other words, we have paid inadequate attention to utilisation of foodgrains. Hence, a more aggressive approach to promote foodgrains consumption by the needy, has to be adopted.

For instance, one could think in terms of paying part of the wages under the Rural Employment Guarantee Scheme in kind, that is, in terms of rice and wheat. We could, thus, be able to greatly enlarge the Employment Schemes themselves. A massive programme of micro watershed development could be launched in the arid regions, with foodgrains being provided as wages for those engaged on these projects.

Food security can be ensured by not merely producing a larger quantum of foodgrains, though this is an essential precondition, but also by facilitating economic access to foodgrains by the needy. That brand of development economics, based on market theology, which only exhorts us to raise the production of foodgrains, without ever bothering to find out the *modus operandi* by which foodgrains so produced reach at least the bulk of the needy is of little relevance to the contemporary Indian economic situation.

Let fiscal experts, and not food management experts, tackle the Centre's budget deficit. There are thousand ways to reduce the deficit. For instance, there is no reason why dividend income should be exempted from income tax. Today, even a person with a crore of rupees dividend income is not taxed: We should subject dividend income to income tax, with an exemption limit of say Rs. 1 lakh. Similarly, in the post-reform era, we are importing gold on an alarming scale, with the average annual imports reaching a figure of $ 5 to $ 6 billion. We could easily impose an import tariff on gold. Measures of this nature will go some way towards reducing the 'high burden' of food subsidy. Essentially, it is a question of reordering of priorities.

6

Redrafting the Agenda for Agricultural Development

False Start

It is now admitted that the process of liberalisation of the Indian economy, introduced through economic reforms initiated in 1991, has largely bypassed the agricultural sector. "Agricultural development must be viewed as a core element of the Plan, since growth in this sector is likely to lead to the widest spread of benefits especially to the rural poor. The first generation of reforms concentrated on the industrial economy and reforms in the agricultural sector were neglected. This must change in the Tenth Plan."[1] What is worse, such reforms as have been actually introduced or contemplated, by contemporary policymakers are mainly inspired by market theology, and are not grounded in the India-specific socio-economic milieu. Hence these reforms have given, as it were, a false start to agricultural development. These reforms constitute a bundle of contradictions. Food subsidy is not consistent with market theology and abolishing it by raising issue prices of foodgrains distributed through the public distribution system (PDS), the minimum support price (MSP) system has resulted in the emergence of large surplus of rice and wheat and hence MSP should be done away with. The cropping pattern should be diversified with a perceptible shift in acreage away from rice and wheat to, say horticultural crops. Huge stocks of foodgrains, mainly rice and wheat, accumulated with the Food Corporation of India (FCI) reaching some 62 million tonnes at one point of time: this was highly embarrassing to policymakers who, alas, did not know what to do with them. They found the easiest way out, by exporting them. Exports of rice and wheat reached an unprecedented level of 11 or 12 million tonnes on 2003-04. Shri Sharad Yadav, the then Minister for Consumer Affairs, Food and

1. *Tenth Five Year Plan, 2002-07,* Vol. I, p. 9.

Public Distribution exults in this achievement: "Today, India has emerged as the world's second largest exporter of rice and the seventh largest exporter of wheat. The country has earned foreign exchange of $ 4 billion through these exports. Though maintaining domestic food security will continue to be top priority, the country's newly-acquired position as a major exporter of foodgrains will be protected."[2]

The Underfed and the Undernourished

It is this agenda for agricultural development drawn up by contemporary policymakers inspired by market theology which needs to be urgently redrafted. Is there a real surplus of foodgrains in today's India? India continues to remain the abode of the largest number of underfed and undernourished persons in the world, despite the high level of production of foodgrains. FAO defines food security as: "the physical economic access for all people at all times for enough food for an active, healthy life, with non-risk of losing such access and as such is directly connected with livelihood in developing countries". The so-called 'surplus', the basic premise on which contemporary policymakers seem to build their strategy for agricultural development, is only 'effective demand surplus' and not a genuine surplus. If domestic food security is to be ensured where is the 'surplus' for exports? In fact, as a consequence of raising the issue prices of foodgrains in the PDS, the off-take of foodgrains declined significantly clearly indicating that foodgrains became increasingly inaccessible to the poorer sections of the population. Even otherwise the per capita availability of cereals actually declined from 450 gms per day in 1991 to 395 gms in 2001. Against this background, exports of foodgrains on a massive scale as in 2003-04 is a travesty of development. Strangely enough, the Tenth Plan which otherwise provides a scholarly analysis of agricultural and food policies, does not make even a casual reference to the mountain of foodgrains co-existing with a mass of underfed population, nor to the targets of reaching food security in a meaningful sense, described above. Even the list of eleven 'Moniterable Targets' of the Tenth Plan does not include the food security target. On the other hand, the Tenth Plan grandiloquently promises: "All villages to have sustained access to potable drinking water within the Plan period."[3] Is it because the Planning Commission experts assume that food security has already been achieved? Would it not have made better sense to ensure food security

2. For excerpts from the Interview with the Minister, *Swagat Magazine*, December 2003.

3. *Tenth Plan*, Volume I, Box 1.1, p. 6.

with foodgrain supplies already available, than to promise potable water which is yet to be made available?

Experts of the Reserve Bank of India (RBI) also seem to believe that we have already attained food security and it is high time we move away from producing rice and wheat to production of high value-added agricultural products such as milk, fruits and vegetables, poultry and fisheries. They hold MSP as the villain of the distorted cropping pattern. "The minimum support price (MSP) policy has distorted the relative prices between rice and wheat, on the one hand, and other food and non-food crops, on the other, giving rise to a distorted cropping pattern. It has contributed to a steep rise in the ratio of procurement to production over the years. The higher increases MSPs of rice and wheat relative to prices of other agricultural commodities has contributed to an incentive structure that favours production of rice and wheat at the cost of other crops. The policy has contributed to a burgeoning stock—far in excess of food security requirements, adding to the carrying costs and locked-in-bank credit, which could have been otherwise deployed for funding productive activities. In view of the associated costs, there is a need for re-examining the price support mechanism to eliminate the distortion of agricultural product composition. In line with diversification of the consumption basket of a representative Indian household, there has been some acceleration in the growth of high value-added agricultural products such as milk, fruits and vegetables, poultry, meat and fisheries during the 1990s. It is essential that this trend is reinforced in the coming years from the viewpoint of enhancing producer incomes and nutrition of consumers. Higher agricultural growth will come from crop diversification to non-traditional activities that are in line with the changing agricultural demand pattern."[4]

While RBI experts' concern for improving the nutrition of consumers is indeed touching, the danger underlying the philosophy of both Government of India and RBI needs to be exposed. Both are trying to push below the carpet the stark reality of a sizeable population continuing to remain in what may be called a state of semi-starvation. According to FAO, more than 225 million Indians remain chronically undernourished and the UNDP estimates that over one-half of all Indian preschoolers suffer from malnutrition. Eliminating hunger should therefore be the first priority on the redrafted agenda of agricultural development. This can be

4. Reserve Bank of India (2003). *Report on Currency and Finance,* 2001-02, March, (page VIII-2).

achieved immediately because fortunately we have been able to successfully generate adequate supplies of foodgrains, mainly rice and wheat. Enriching the consumer basket of the relatively better-off thus becomes a priority of the second order. We must first look at those consumers whose baskets are practically or nearly empty.

Conventional wisdom stipulates that the problem of poverty can be tackled through higher GDP growth, expansion of employment and generation of supplementary income through secondary occupations and soon. But the process is a long haul and may take at least two decades, as the recent experience of China has demonstrated. The Tenth Plan which has analysed the trends in poverty reinforces this conclusion clearly the mandated reduction in poverty rate of 5 percentage points during the Tenth Plan and another 10 percentage points during the Eleventh Plan will still leave more than 11 per cent of the population or about 130 million people below the poverty line in 2012. It is as if the policymakers are throwing up their hands declaring that the situation is hopeless. Do the contemporary policymakers expect the "semi-starving India", to remain with us always?

In the redrafted agenda therefore the approach should be: In the India-specific unique situation, plan to eliminate hunger first and poverty later. The co-existence of embarrassingly large stocks of foodgrains with FCI and sizeable unsatisfied demand for foodgrains is an anachronism. Policy makers should grow out of their market theology and address the issue head-long. In any other country, such a situation would have exploded into a revolution. Ours is an ancient civilization known for its quiescence. Exporting of a small quantity of high-value branded commodity like *Basamati* rice is certainly welcome, but massive exports of 10 to 12 million tonnes of ordinary quality rice and wheat is totally unwarranted. What is worse, our exports of foodgrains are highly subsidised. For instance, during the four years 2000-01 to 2003-04, the price realised on rice exports has been generally lower than the issue prices of rice provided to families below the poverty line (BPL). This is taking the 'export optimism' to its absurd heights. In other words, the same market theologists who are advocating the abolition of domestic food subsidy are encouraging subsidising foreign consumers of Indian foodgrains! Food policy has thus become a bundle of contradictions. To reiterate, we need all the cereals we produce for domestic consumption and in fact, the rate of production of cereals needs to be accelerated. Even modest projections of demand for cereals in 2020 place the estimate at 260 million tonnes, as compared to the production level of 187 million tonnes in 2001. The enormous gap between demand and supply is thus obvious. Logically therefore the incentive mechanism to promote production of rice and wheat—the MSP, procurement of foodgrains by FCI and the public distribution system must also be reinforced. This does mean that there is no scope for modification or rationalisation of this mechanism. The point is that market theologists should be warned of the grave dangers to food security, if this incentive mechanism is dismantled on the specious ground of 'Surpluses' of foodgrains. Our policymakers should disabuse their mind of the illusion of 'Surpluses'. RBI experts, quoted earlier, have an important point. We do need to produce more fruits and vegetables, milk, poultry and fisheries products, etc. But this is not an 'either or' proposition. We do not have to cut down our acreage under rice and wheat to be able to produce other products. There is enough scope to raise the production of these products without impinging on the production of cereals. For instance, some states like Maharashtra have made in more recent years remarkable progress in horticulture without encroaching upon the production of cereals. The substitution of rice/wheat by horticultural crops could, at best, be marginal. In fact the thrust for growth of agriculture and allied activities must emanate in the coming years, from agriculture in its extended sense, particularly the livestock sub-sector, which holds out great promise for growth. The extended arms of the agricultural sector should, therefore, receive greater prominence in the redrafted agenda.

Reaching Food to the Poor

The tragedy of Indian planning is that, over the years, we have developed the technology and the institutional framework to produce adequate quantities of foodgrains or cereals at any rate, but we simply do not know how to reach the foodgrains so produced to the needy. The muddle-headedness of food management policy discussed earlier reflects this tragedy. Food security in a meaningful sense is ensured not merely by producing adequate quantum of foodgrains but also by reaching the food to the needy. The latter task is inextricably interwoven with the livelihood or employment, because a majority of the poor is not only asset-less but also without any assured or continuous employment. This brings to the employment situation.

The current backlog of unemployment is around 9 per cent or equivalent to 35 million persons and thus is far too high. This is on top of the large underemployment or disguised unemployment. On the basis of the Prime Minister's vision of creating 100 million employment opportunities over the next 10 years, the Tenth Plan has set a target of creation of 50 million jobs during the next five years. If this target is achieved, unemployment is likely to decline to some 5 per cent by the end of the Tenth Plan. To be able to realise the target, the focus will have to be on a wide range of sectors such as agriculture and allied sectors, construction, tourism, transport, small scale industries (SSIs), retailing, etc. To facilitate growth in these sectors, supportive policies need to be put in place. Here is the rub.

Public sector banks have failed even today to meet the credit target of 18 per cent of net bank credit to agriculture, the actual level being some 15 per cent in 2002-03. PSBs should enhance their presence in the rural sector with a view to facilitating not only faster agricultural growth, but also a wide range of activities in the non-farm sector, self-employment, retail trade, services and generally decentralised development. One has to foster decentralised growth of a multitude of microenterprises in the rural and semi-urban sector, the Chinese experience is illuminating in this context. To facilitate such broad-based growth we have to organise and build Self-Help Groups (SHGs), micro-credit institutions, and increasingly seek to involve NGOs in the process. It is encouraging to note that RBI has begun to take recently some initiatives in this direction. While on this subject, it is refreshing to note that the Exim Bank has recently identified the agriculture and processed food sector as a thrust sector in its business strategy. It has identified certain products as having maximum export potential[5] and has started financing export oriented contract farming and organic farming and related activities. One hopes PSBs and NABARD would emulate this example in their respective areas.

Employment expansion is an ideal way by which the poor would be empowered to have access to foodgrains. This method needs to be supplemented by other modalities to achieve the objective in the immediate run: linking of rural development works like micro watershed development programmes to utilisation of foodgrains, instituting "Grain Loans Facility" for all institutions involved in financing rural development programmes like rural co-operatives, RRBs, even NGOs. I have spelt out these possibilities elsewhere.[6] There is also the need to activate the mid-

5. The identified products include frozen shrimp, prawns, coffee (green and not decaf) fresh grapes, melon, papayas, avocado, guava, mangoes, malt extract, oil cakes of soybean, raw cane sugar, dried and shelled chickpeas, whole cloves, garlic, bovine meat, sheep meat and black tea.

6. Mujumdar, N.A. (2002). "Rural Development: New Perceptions", *Economic and Political Weekly*, September 28.

day meal schemes to provide children in government and government assisted primary schools with prepared meals. This scheme confers multiple benefits to the economy. In fact universal and nutritious mid-day meals would be a great leap forward toward the realisation of right to food. The main point to drive home is that productive utilisation of all the foodgrain domestically—and not through exports—should the dominant objective of development policy subsuming all other objectives.

The founding fathers of the Indian Society of Agricultural Economics had in their wisdom inscribed in the Society's logo the following motto: "*Dhan Dhanyam Vipulam Bhavatu*", or "Let there be surpluses of wealth and foodgrains". We have achieved this objective because our foreign exchange reserves have soared to the unprecedented level of beyond $ 100 billion and we have been living with the so-called foodgrains surpluses, for the past 3 or 4 years, the food stocks with FCI, at one point, exceeding 60 million tonnes. Little did these forefathers realise that contemporary policy makers in the 1990s and early 2000s, soaked in the market theology would frustrate the cherished objective of ensuring adequate food to all in the country, by exporting large quantities of foodgrains. The redrafting of the agenda for agricultural development has therefore become imperative. We ave now to pursue food security in the holistic sense. It is not enough to produce adequate quantities of foodgrains: it is also necessary to ensure that foodgrains so produced reach all the needy. If this extended concept of food security is to be achieved, agricultural development itself assumes different connotations. Employment must be expanded not only in agriculture but also in a allied sectors like livestock. Investment in agriculture does not end with investment in large and medium irrigation projects: but it would also involve pursuit of micro watershed development projects on a massive scale and rain water harvesting. Empowering the rural poor through employment expansion, both wage-paid and self-employment, so as to enable them to access foodgrains should constitute an integral part of agriculture development strategy. Of course, these programmes need to be supplemented with special programmes aimed at benefiting specific target groups like school-going children.

Conclusion

The starting point of the redrafted agenda would therefore be that there are no exportable surpluses of foodgrains: what we observe today as surplus stocks are effective demand surpluses. For ensuring meaningful food security, it is not enough to produce adequate quantities of foodgrains: it is also necessary to ensure that these foodgrains reach the needy and the poor. This holistic concept of food security assumes greater significance because removal of poverty is a long haul. Even if the targeted reduction in poverty is achieved, as stipulated in the Tenth and Eleventh Plans, about 130 million persons would continue to remain poor by 2012. In terms of 'immediacy' therefore, providing minimum foodgrains in terms of caloric requirements becomes a viable alternative as a 'second best' solution. India cannot afford, at this stage, to institute a comprehensive social security scheme on the lines of those prevalent in say the UK or the USA. Through the various modalities discussed earlier and with appropriate supportive policies in place, India can atleast seek to guarantee the right to food to all it citizens.

7

Watershed Development

Mother of All Water Management Modes

Food Security

The announcement made by the Government of India this month that India will import 'initially' half a million tonnes of wheat rings a warning bell. What about the oft-repeated pronouncements by policymakers that India has attained self-sufficiency in foodgrains? Or, the more brazen claim by the Government of India's Economic Survey 2003-2004: "The Government's special efforts to encourage exports of foodgrains in recent years through grant of World Trade Organization (WTO) compatible subsidies has placed India as one of the leading exporters of foodgrains in the international market."[1] These statements have been reduced to empty rhetorics. In fact, the logic underlying such statements is itself flawed, as I have spelt out elsewhere.[2]

The hard reality is that we need to produce foodgrains on a much larger scale to meet fully domestic consumption requirements, for instance, food production needs to be raised to 250 million tonnes by 2025. The Tenth Plan (2002-2007) target of agricultural growth is an annual average of 4 per cent. In reality, the annual average for the first three years of the Plan was a dismal 1.1 per cent. Even during the year 2005-06 when the GDP growth soared to 8.1 per cent, agricultural growth was only 2.3 per cent. Something seems to be basically wrong with our approach for agricultural growth. Accelerating agricultural growth has thus, acquired a sense of sinister urgency.

What are the options open to us? Large and medium irrigation projects? Or, green revolution? Both of these have to be ruled out in the

---

1. Government of India (2004). *Economic Survey 2003-04*, New Delhi, p. 106.
2. See ch. 2 of this book.

immediate run. We would seek to argue here that watershed development; both macro and micro, seems to be the only feasible solution to increasing foodgrains production in the immediate run. That is why we have called watershed development as the mother of all water management modes. In the short run, therefore, watershed development should be the dominant strategy for accelerating agricultural growth.

Large Irrigation Projects

Historically, the overriding compulsion of attaining self-sufficiency in foodgrains has driven the development of irrigation in India. This strategy of treating irrigation projects—mainly large and medium—as the kingpin of agricultural growth has paid rich dividends: nearly 60 per cent of the crop output now originates from irrigated area, which accounts for about 40 per cent of the total cropped area. This approach was perhaps appropriate in the historical context but the present situation is quite different. If the large and medium irrigation potential is fully exploited, it may be possible to raise the per cent of irrigated area to 70. But investment in irrigation is grossly inadequate because the states do not simply have the resources required. Some idea of the massive investment requirements can be had from the fact that completion of all ongoing projects alone is estimated to cost around Rs. 1,00,000 crore.[3] This is exclusive of new irrigation projects. Then there is an inordinately long time lag. According to Dr. Ahluwalia of the Planning Commission, at the present rate of incremental addition to irrigated area, it will take 30 years to complete all the ongoing large and medium irrigation projects.[4] Surely, the country cannot afford to wait 30 years to become self-sufficient in foodgrains!

Second Green Revolution

Recently, Prime Minister Dr. Manmohan Singh called for a second Green Revolution: "I believe we do need a second Green Revolution in agriculture...based on the application of new technologies and modern business practices. New technology will enable farmers to make more informed choices and undertake product planning in a demand driven

3. Ahluwalia, S. Montek (2006). "Reducing Poverty and Hunger in India: The Role of Agriculture", *Annual Report 2004-2005*, International Food Policy Research Institute, Washington, D.C.

4. Ahluwalia, S. Montek (2006). "Agricultural Situation: Policies for Achieving Production Increases in Indian Agriculture", *Economic Developments in India*, Vol. 93, Academic Foundation, New Delhi, p. 57.

rather than supply-driven mode."[5] Jeffrey Sachs, who has emerged as a modern development *guru*, has endorsed the Prime Minister's statement. "Agriculture has not done well. The Prime Minister is right when he says that a second Green Revolution, is needed but in poorer areas."[6] While another Green Revolution would indeed be welcome, we wonder whether genetic breakthrough of the Borlug type can be made to order, as it were.

Vision of Agricultural Growth

Three important points emerge from the analysis of the current macro agronomic situation. First, since a large part of our cultivable area is rainfed, and will continue to remain rainfed even when the full irrigation potential is exploited, the focus of agricultural development policy will have to be on these rainfed areas. Second, relying on large and medium irrigation projects to increase foodgrains production substantially would be futile because of the long time lags involved. Third, our vision of agricultural growth in the new millennium would have to be such that it achieves the broader objectives of less capital-intensive growth, employment-led growth, and growth which results in food security for all and in poverty reduction. In future, therefore, greater emphasis will have to be placed on agriculture in rainfed or dry-regions, where there is concentration of poverty and food insecurity.

Water-Centric Growth

Of course, agricultural development in future will have, also, to be necessarily water-centric because large tracts of dry lands are involved. The only difference is that as contradistinguished from our empirical experience of depending primarily on large and medium irrigation projects, we have to think of other options. There is a need for out-of-box thinking. Four interconnected programmes assume significance in this context: watershed development programmes, both micro and macro; renovation of all water bodies linked to agriculture, which have presently fallen into disuse; correcting the deterioration of public irrigation works, notably state canal systems, due to cumulative neglect of repair and maintenance over the years; and rainwater harvesting; despite reasonable rainfall in large parts of the country, we seem to be concentrating on mining water rather than harvesting our water resources.

---

5. Singh, Manmohan (2005). "Second Green Revolution in Indian Agriculture", Inaugural Address at the Agricultural Summit, organised by FICCI and the Ministry of Agriculture, New Delhi, April 9, 2005; *Economic Developments in India*, Vol. 89, Academic Foundation, New Delhi, p. 21.

6. Interview with Jeffrey Sachs, *Times of India*, February 6, 2006.

Historically, Indian agriculture has been sustained by natural and man-made water bodies such as tanks, lakes, ponds and similar structures. There are more than a million such structures, of which about 50,000 are utilised for irrigation. Many of them have fallen into disuse, accumulating silt and these need to be restored urgently. The Budget for 2004-05 prepared a massive scheme to repair, renovate, and restore all these water bodies directly linked to agriculture. A pilot project one in each district was launched at an estimated outlay of Rs. 100 crore. This is indeed a good beginning in an entirely neglected area.

Secondly, maintaining the canal systems in good shape is important to derive full benefits from irrigation. The performance of many states in this area leaves much to be desired. Poor maintenance leads to loss of water through seepage, with the result that water use efficiency is very low—around 25 to 40 per cent, as against the 65 per cent which is attainable. Irrigation departments of states plead lack of resources for poor maintenance.

Today, watershed development is seen as the principal strategy for holistic development of rainfed areas, though in the initial stages it was conceived mainly as a measure for moisture conservation and soil stabilisation. The 'Watershed Plus' approach to watershed development as spelt out in the Tenth Plan seeks to ensure convergence of all other programmes that promote economic activities and generate increased employment opportunities. Moreover, rainwater conservation and harvesting confers two-fold benefits: in addition to use for current crops, it has important implications for the groundwater crisis that the country is facing due to 'indiscriminate use of tubewell technology in parts of the country. The Samaj Pragati Sahayog which has been working on watershed projects across 50 districts in 5 states, Madhya Pradesh, Chhattisgarh, Jharkhand, Bihar and Rajasthan has accumulated interesting experience in this sphere. "We find that drastic improvements are possible in groundwater levels due to harvesting of rainwater. The mud dams we make are like the current account that must be used, while keeping the capital account of groundwater safe in the bank. For rainwater harvesting to be effective, careful attention must be paid to the uses to which the water is put. Water 'intensive' crops must not be grown in drought-prone areas. Farmers must adopt drip irrigation."[7]

---

7. "Water Warrior", *Times of India*, March 27, 2004.

Genesis of Watershed Development

In fact, watershed development programmes are not new to India and they have a fairly long history. It was in 1986 that the National Water Development Project for Rainfed Areas (NWDPRA) covering 99 districts in 16 states was introduced.[8] Initially this programme was focused on growth and stabilisation of ecosystem balance. After three years of implementation of watershed development programme, a Committee was appointed to review the guidelines prepared at the time of introduction of NWDPRA. This Committee revised the guidelines, widening the scope of the programme. The revised guidelines published in 1992 came to be known as Watershed Area Rainfed Agricultural System Approach (WARASAD), which had five-fold objectives including, generation of employment, reduction of inequalities between irrigated and rainfed areas.

A number of researchers have evaluated the ecological and economic impact of these watershed development programmes. "A vast majority of studies not only confirmed the economic viability of the programme but also indicated the fact that watershed programme is the *only* alternative to development of rainfed agriculture in India"[8] (emphasis supplied).

In spite of these unanimous findings, one begins to wonder why has the programme not caught on. On the whole, the achievements are patchy. Even in Maharashtra which is the pioneering state in this field, only 15 per cent of the eligible area is covered by the programme. There are some success stories like Ralgaon Siddhi in Maharashtra or the work of Samaj Pragati Sahayog referred to above. But what is needed is universalisation or near universalisation of the programme with the objective of covering the bulk of the rainfed area.

One of the reasons for lack of enthusiasm could be that watershed development programmes are not spectacular like say, the Bhakra-Nangal irrigation project. Hence, they do not appeal to bureaucrats or politicians. Secondly, these involve a lot of organisational effort at the grassroots level: involving the village *Panchayat*, designing the programme at the village level and so on.

But this must change. Massive watershed development programme, both micro and macro, seem to be the only alternative which satisfies most of the conditionalities we are seeking: it is less capital intensive, particularly at the micro level. It serves the multiple objectives of

---

8. Raju, K.V. *et al.* (2004). "Water Resources", Vol. 3, *State of the Indian Farmer—A Millennium Study*, Academic Foundation, New Delhi.

agricultural growth, which we have spelt out earlier: it enhances employment opportunities and reduces poverty, and offers food security to these who need it most. Equally important is the test of 'immediacy'. These programmes do not have long gestation periods.

Conclusion

We should, therefore, adopt watershed development as a dominant strategy for agricultural development in the coming years. For instance, the objective should be to cover say, 50 per cent of the eligible area in the next two years. Only such a massive programme can make a perceptible impact on food production. Secondly, we should adopt a holistic approach to watershed development. For example, if deforestation problems upstream are not tackled, water retention structures downstream will quickly silt up. Similarly, the Rural Employment Guarantee Scheme could be made to subserve the watershed development programme. The 73rd Constitutional Amendment incorporates soil conservation and agriculture in its schedule 11, thus, transferring the power to village *panchayats* in this regard. Hence, village *panchayats* can accord priority to watershed development schemes, under the Rural Employment Guarantee Programmes. Involving the potential beneficiaries in the implementation of the micro watershed development project would be useful. Similarly, micro watershed development schemes could be partly financed under the food-for-work programmes. Thus, if all the other relevant programmes converge on the watershed development projects, it should be possible to successfully implement a massive watershed development programme.

Let there be no misunderstanding. It is certainly not my intention to de-emphasise problems of large and medium irrigation projects. Or, to ignore important issues of discouraging wasteful use or over-use of water in some parts of the country. Similarly, the critical role of water charges and power rates in discouraging excess use of groundwater needs to recognised. There is also the need to promote greater water-use efficiency through measures like drip irrigation. In any discussions on water management, all these issues need to be examined in depth.

All that I have sought to highlight is that given the present food security situation of the country, the dominant strategy for agricultural growth in the immediate run, should be through promotion of watershed development schemes, both micro and macro. These schemes are less capital intensive. They generate employment and they result in ensuring food security to those who need it most. Although the economic impact of such schemes is well established, they have not attracted adequate attention of policymakers or bureaucrats perhaps because they are mundane and not glamorous. But as some evaluation studies have shown, perhaps there is no alternative to these schemes for the dry areas. The sooner we launch such schemes on a massive scale, the better it would be for food security for those who need it most.

8

Rural Employment

Beyond the Monetary and Fiscal Arithmetic

The poor in India seem to be doomed forever. In the 1960s when India went through the wretchedness of absolute shortages of foodgrains, of course, the poor could not access foodgrains because of high prices. The average annual imports of wheat were as high as 3 million tonnes. Towards the end of the 1990s, India entered the era of the so-called foodgrains 'surpluses'. The stocks of foodgrains with the Food Corporation of India (FCI) soared, at one point of time, to 60 million tonnes. Embarrassed by the huge surpluses, the Government of India sought a way out by exporting foodgrains on a massive scale: exports of foodgrains exceeded 10 million tonnes in 2003-04. India is the abode of the largest number of underfed and undernourished people in the world. How does one explain the coexistence of large 'surpluses' of foodgrains with large unsatisfied domestic demand for foodgrains? Should not elimination of hunger be the primordial priority in the hierarchy of development objectives? If so, how does one reconcile the massive exports of foodgrains? The net result is that the poor had to go without food, even during years of 'surpluses' as during years of shortages.

For a predominently agricultural country like India, it was tragic enough not being able to produce adequate quantity of foodgrains in the 1960s. More tragic is perhaps the situation in the late 1990s or early 2000s: Having achieved the herculean task of producing adequate quantum of foodgrains, Indian policymakers are not able to reach these grains to the needy and the poor. This is a reflection of not so much their intellectual infirmity as of intellectual servility.

In part, the anomaly of the poor not being able to access foodgrains even during years of surpluses is explained by the fact that contemporary Indian policymakers are soaked in the neo-classical market theology of IMF and World Bank. They would like to do away with food subsidies, which in turn means raising the issue prices of foodgrains distributed through the public distribution system (PDS). Thus, foodgrains have become increasingly inaccessible to the poor. Strange enough, the same policy-makers have no compunction in subsidising foreign consumers of Indian foodgrains. Because our exports of foodgrains are highly subsidised. The *Economic Survey 2003-2004* boasts: "The Governments' special efforts to encourage export of foodgrains in recent years through grant of WTO compatible subsidies have placed India as one of the leading exporters of foodgrains in the international market" (page 166).

Contemporary Indian policymakers seem to conveniently forget that India has no social security schemes of the type prevalent in the developed countries like the UK or the USA. Even a developing country like Sri Lanka has *Samurdhi*, a major poverty alleviation programme of the Government, which has been in operation since 1995, providing cash relief (a monthly relief allowance) to more than 2 million families.

The only asset that the poor has is labour and hence, perhaps the only way of empowering the poor to access foodgrains is through providing employment. The National Rural Employment Guarantee Act 2004 (NREGA) was tabled in Parliament on 21st December, 2004. The Bill seeks to provide guaranteed employment at the statutory minimum wage to at least one adult per rural household, who volunteers to do casual manual labour. To begin with, the scheme would cover 150 most backward districts—districts which are covered by food-for-work programme. By limiting the scheme to 150 districts, the annual expenditure on the scheme would be contained well within Rs. 10,000 crore, whereas if the programme was spread throughout the country, the expenditure would have soared to Rs. 25,000 crore.

Already, the scheme has aroused sufficient resentment particularly from those intellectuals brought up on the diet of market theology of IMF/World Bank. The Economic Times in its editorial states vociferously that the scheme will cause "fiscal stress, feed inflation, hurt growth, and worsen the condition of the poor. Growth is what the poor need, to get out of poverty. It would be the worst irony if providing temporary relief in the state of poverty were to derail growth that offers emancipation from poverty" (20 December, 2004).

It has become fashionable to speak of emancipation of poverty through growth. It is alright for management gurus like C.K. Prahlad to talk of eradication of poverty through profits. But they are blissfully oblivious of the time-scale. What is the ground reality? For instance, even if India were to sustain a GDP growth of 7 or 8 per cent in the Tenth Plan, the poverty reduction would be only by 5 per cent. Another 10 percentage points reduction in poverty is stipulated in the Eleventh Plan. Even assuming the growth is sustained as envisaged in the two Plans, this will still leave more than 11 per cent of the population or about 130 million people below the poverty line in 2012. Thus, poverty reduction through the normal process of growth, as envisaged by the market theologists is a long haul. Do these policymakers expect the "Semi-Starving India", if one might use the term, to always remain with us? And that too, when we have adequate supplies of foodgrains to feed them? These are disturbing questions indeed which market experts should address first before condemning the Rural Employment Scheme.

Secondly, the apprehension of these experts that this scheme which involves injection of say, Rs. 10,000 crore in the economy, would lead to inflation is also misplaced. This apprehension only reflects the fact that we continue to be slaves of the crude quantity theory of money. In the Indian situation, it is possible to contain inflation within a reasonable band, if we have adequate supplies of 'wage-goods', mainly food and textiles. We have enough of these supplies and this is further buttressed by robust foreign exchange reserves which have soared to historically high levels. In case of shortage of edible oil, for instance, we can import it. Given such strong supply side, it is possible to contain inflation irrespective of what the monetary or fiscal arithmetic would indicate. It is useful to recollect here that in the early years of the Planning era, we had evolved the concept of 'safe level of deficit financing' India's resource endowments of today are unique and no standard textbook can guide us in terms of how to make the best out of this configuration of circumstances. Elimination of poverty through the market theology induced growth is a long haul. On the other hand, we can eliminate hunger now through employment generation. Poverty elimination can afford to wait, but not hunger elimination. Thus, the rural employment scheme meets the test of 'immediacy'.

This is certainly not to argue that the Rural Employment Scheme proposed to be implemented is perfect. In fact, the scheme would have been a more effective, if the Government of India were to declare the year 2005 as a 'Year of Watershed Development' and all the rural labour would have been deployed on the related schemes of water harvesting and conservation in rainfed areas. Since these areas are the abode of the bulk of the poor, the targeting would have been more appropriate. State Governments do not seem to be exactly enthusiastic about such rural employment schemes which are far from being glamorous. This is clearly reflected in the fact that the utilisation of foodgrains by States under the food-for-work scheme is very poor. Although foodgrains are provided free of cost by the Centre to the States, the latter do not seem to be keen to fully utilise the foodgrains. Perhaps involving Panchayati Raj institutions in designing and implementation of the rural employment schemes would go some way to reap greater benefits from the schemes.

Overall, in judging the usefulness of the rural employment scheme, one has to look beyond monetary and fiscal arithmetic and consider what development objective can be realised by effectively implementing the rural employment programme.

9

Millennium Development Goals and Development Policies

Recently there seems to have been a revival of interest, among international institutions, in poverty and food security. The recent ODI Report on "Fighting Poverty in Africa: Are PRSPs Making a Difference" and FAO Report on "The State of Food Security in the World 2004: Monitoring Progress Towards the World Food Summit and Millennium Development Goals" are instances in point. The UN Report on "Investing in Development: A Practical Plan to achieve the Millennium Development Goals" (New York, 2005) belongs to this genre.

It may be recalled that at the Millennium Summit in September 2000, "the largest gathering of world leaders in history adopted the UN Millennium Declaration, committing their nations to a new global partnership to reduce poverty, improve health and promote peace, human rights, gender equality, and environmental sustainability" (p.3). The Millennium Development Goals, an off-shoot of the above Declaration, are the world's time bound and quantified targets for addressing extreme poverty in its many dimensions—income, poverty, hunger, disease, lack of shelter—while promoting gender equality, education and environmental sustainability. The Goals set some 18 targets which include: (i) halve, between 1990 and 2015, the proportion of people whose income is less than $ 1 a day; (ii) halve, between 1990 and 2015, the proportion of people who suffer from hunger; (iii) ensure that, by 2015, children every where, boys and girls alike, will be able to complete a full course of primary schooling; (iv) reduce by two-thirds, between 1990 and 2015, the under-five mortality rate; (v) halve, by 2015, the proportion of people without sustainable access to safe drinking water and basic sanitation, and (vi) in co-operation with developing countries, develop and implement strategies for decent and productive work for youth.

The Report asserts that these Goals, "drive a new era in international development. They are the first, international goals to recognise at the highest political level, that poverty in the poorest countries can be dramatically reduced only if developing countries put well designed and well implemented plans in place to reduce poverty—and only if rich countries match their effort with substantial increases in support. No well intended but impoverished country is to be left under 'business as usual', solely to its own resources" (p.4).

The UN Millennium Project is an independent advisory body commissioned by the UN to evolve best strategies for meeting the Millennium Development Goals (MDGs). The Project was directed by Professor Jeffrey D. Sachs and the bulk of the analytical work was carried out by 10 thematic task forces comprising more than 250 experts from around the world, including scientists, development economists and practitioners. Dr. M.S. Swaminathan was one of the Task Force Coordinators. The Report of 329 pages which is the result of these massive efforts, is divided into three Parts: While Part 1 explains why MDGs are important, Part 2 spells out country-level processes to achieve MDGs. Part 3 makes recommendations for the international system to support the country-level processes outlined in Part 2.

The reviewer feels that the most valuable contribution of the Report is the insight it provides into the development process through cross-country experiences. "While progress in China and India is to be lauded as a global-scale triumph, it would be a mistake to declare 'victory' in cutting extreme poverty on the basis of progress mainly in two countries, while dozens of other countries with hundreds of millions of the World's poorest people are not meeting the Goals" (p.3). The Report is particularly ecstatic about China. "China's economic performance in the last two decades has been nothing short of spectacular" (p.159). Real per capita income growth averaged 8.2 per cent per year. The incidence of rural poverty declined from 30 per cent in 1990 to 11 per cent in 2002. China would therefore be able to reach the MDGs. The Report commends India's economic performance over the past decade as 'strong' (p.163). Per capita income growth was around 4 per cent per year. The percentage of people below the poverty line dropped from 37.5 per cent in 1990 to 26 per cent in 2000. But India faces several challenges in meeting other Goals: high rates of under nutrition, large number of children out of school, poor health indicators, wide disparities in social and economic indicators, particularly for women and disadvantaged sections of the population.

India's most pressing challenge, according to the Report, is a massive scaling up of public investments in the rural areas of the worst performing States (p.165). An MDG-based investment strategy for India is therefore recommended. For the Indian researcher this is the all too familiar ground and there is little 'value addition' to the existing knowledge on the subject.

Take the countries of East Asia. As a Group, it has moved closer to achieving the Goals but progress has been uneven within the region. The Report illustrates the disparities by contrasting the performance of Thailand and Cambodia. Thailand, a high performer, was able to reduce poverty from 27.2 per cent of the population in 1990 to 9.8 per cent in 2002. The proportion of underweight children dropped from 18.6 per cent to 8.5 per cent. There was significant progress in achieving other Goals also. By contrast, despite commitment to MDGs, Cambodia is off track for most Goals (p.161). It would have been helpful if the Report were to throw some light on the factors underlying the contrasting performances.

Turning to Africa, the Report poses the question: Why has progress toward the MDGs proved so difficult in much of Sub-Saharan Africa? The standard diagnosis is that the continent is suffering from a governance crisis. But the Report argues that this is a superficial explanation. "Our explanation is that tropical Africa, even in well governed parts, is stuck in a poverty trap—too poor to achieve robust and high levels of economic growth, and in many places simply too poor to grow at all. More policy or governance reform, by itself, is not sufficient to break out of this trap. Africa's extreme poverty leads to low national savings rates, which in turn lead to low or negative economic growth rates" (p.148). The average saving rate in tropical Sub-Saharan Africa is about 11 per cent, as compared to 20 per cent in Latin America or 18 per cent in South Asia or 34 per cent in East Asia and the Pacific. The combination of low domestic saving rate and high population growth has led to stagnation in Africa. This brief discussion gives some flavour of the useful insights into the development process one might gain by browsing through the Report.

On a broader canvass, two aspects of the likely impact that this Report may make on development economics and policy in general may be highlighted. First, the market theology of the IMF and the World Bank had greatly influenced public policy in many developing countries in the 1990s. The mindless pursuit of market-led growth strategies had diluted the development content of public policy. Indian policymakers of the 1990s perhaps were no exception. A correction of this euphoria of market-led growth was overdue. This Report provides the correction in a subtle manner. Recommendation I of the Report stipulates: "Developing country governments should adopt development strategies bold enough to meet the Millennium Development Goal (MDG) targets for 2015. We term them MDG-based poverty reduction strategies. To meet the 2015 deadline, we recommend that all countries have these strategies in place by 2006. Where Poverty Reduction Strategy Papers (PRPs) already exist, these should be aligned with MDGs" (p.XX). By making MDGs as the focal point of public policy, the Report has succeeded in bringing on the top of the development agenda issues like reduction of poverty, elimination of hunger, health and education of the rural poor. Direct attack on poverty had become anathema to policy makers during the market theology phase, but it has now again become respectable. This is indeed a remarkable achievement. Interestingly enough, in the case of India, the National Common Minimum Programme (CMP) of the present UPA Government clearly reflects this changed perception of development.

The second aspect relates to what the Report calls 'global partnership for an inter-connected world', between rich and poor nations. Recommendation 7 stipulates: "High-income countries should increase official development assistance (ODA) from 0.25 per cent of donor GNP in 2003 to around 0.44 per cent in 2006 and 0.54 in 2015 to support the Millennium Development Goals, particularly in low-income countries with improved ODA quality (including aid that is harmonised, predictable and largely in the form of grant-based budget support)" (p.XXII). How far is this target achievable? It has become necessary to pose this question because past record in this area is disappointing. Those with long memory would recall that the World Bank had appointed a Commission under the Chairmanship of Lester Pearson, a former Prime Minister of Canada, to make an in-depth study of aid for development and make recommendations for facilitating larger flow of aid. The Commission's Report submitted in 1969, entitled 'Partners in Development' was acclaimed, at that point of time, as "one of the most important documents of the twentieth century."[1] The Commission had recommended that the commitment of official development assistance (ODA) should "reach 0.70 per cent of GNP by 1975 or shortly thereafter, but in no case later than 1980." This target must be compared with the average flow of 0.39 per cent in 1968. Alas, are we trading in 2005 on the same ground as in

1. Mujumdar, N.A. (1969). "Unequal Partners in Development", *Economic and Political Weekly*, November 22.

1969? Or, are the circumstances in 2005 any different? The present Report advances one additional factor "Many world leaders have stressed the fact that the fight for global security—to stop war, internal violence, terror and other ills of profound instability—requires success in the battle against poverty as well" (p. 10). The modern breed of terrorism is not necessarily poverty-born. Moreover, this is tantamount to assuming that the rich donor countries would prefer tackling the factors like poverty which have the potential to sow terrorism, to spending more on arms to suppress terrorism. The reviewer for one, is not sure whether this is a realistic assumption. Instead, the rich donor countries should be inspired by the concept of "shared growth" which characterised the growth process, at the national level, in the Asian Tiger countries. Applied at the international level, this concept could inspire a more meaningful partnership between rich donor countries and the poor countries. One can only hope that the Sachs Report recommendations will not meet the same fate as those of the Pearson Commission.

10

Unequal Partners in Development

An air of general scepticism surrounds the question of aid to developing countries now a days. The very usefulness of aid, both to the donors and the recipients, is being questioned. The World Bank thought, therefore, that the wide range of problems relating to aid needed to be examined afresh and, with this objective, it appointed in August 1968 a Commission under the Chairmanship of Lester Pearson, a former Prime Minister of Canada, to undertake such a study. In addition to the Chairman, the Commission consisted of seven[1] distinguished persons drawn from different walks of life, and it included Arthur Lewis. The Report[2] of the Commission, extending to 400 pages, was presented to the Annual Meeting of the World Bank in Washington on October 1, 1969. It has already been acclaimed 'one of the most important documents of the twentieth century'. The purpose of this article is to examine the more important of the recommendations of the Commission and to indicate briefly the impact that the Report is likely to have on the inflow of aid to developing countries.

Trends in Aid and Trade

Judged in absolute terms, the total net financial flows, public and private, from the developed countries to the developing countries have expanded steadily in recent years. For instance, total net capital flows from DAC[3] countries to the developing countries rose from $ 9.2 billion in 1961 to $ 12.8 billion in 1968 (Table 10.1). However, judged as a

---

1. Parenthetically, it may be added that although no Indian was a member of the Commission, of the 22 consultants listed on the last page of the Report, 7 were drawn from India.

2. *Partners in Development*, Praeger Paperbacks, New York, 1969.

3. Members of the Development Association Committee of the Organisation for Economic Co-operation and Development: participants are Australia, Austria, Belgium, Canada, Denmark, France, Germany, Italy, Japan, the Netherlands, Norway, Portugal, Sweden, Switzerland, UK, USA, and EEC Commission.

proportion of the GNP of the DAC countries, the quantum of flows shows an actual decline. While the capital flow formed nearly 1 per cent of the combined GNP of DAC countries in 1961, this percentage declined to 0.75 in 1968. In this relative sense, therefore, the aid flow has actually contracted.[4]

Table 10.1

Total Net Flow of Resources to Developing Countries and Multilateral Agencies

(Billions in US $)

	1961	*1963*	*1967*	*1968*
Total	9.2	8.6	11.2	12.8
Official Development Assistance Flows	5.2	5.9	6.6	6.4
Grant and Grant-like Contributions	4.5	4.4	4.4	4.1
Loans	0.6	1.5	2.3	2.4
Other Official Flows	0.9	0.2	0.3	0.5
Private Flows	3.1	2.5	4.2	5.8

In part, the contraction is attributable to the domestic economic problems of the developed countries. For instance, in 1968, the major concern in many of these countries was about the restraining of the buoyancy of their economies, both by monetary and fiscal measures. There was, as a consequence, a marked decline in the official flows of capital in 1968, especially from the UK and the USA. Further, looking at the picture from the point of view of future trends, the net flow of official assistance may tend to decline in the coming years, in view of the sharp cuts in recent years in the US foreign economic assistance appropriations: the US alone accounts for almost one-half of the total of official and private flows from all DAC countries.

Turning to the trade aspect, the export earnings of the developing countries have a crucial influence on their import capacity and their development potential. Thus, although trade is not a substitute for foreign aid, it is important to underscore that the need for aid arises partly from the inadequacy of the foreign exchange earnings of the developing countries and the difficulties of sizeably increasing these earnings. The

4. Financial flows from non-DAC countries have been relatively modest.

trend in the developing countries' share of the world trade therefore, becomes relevant. World exports, excluding the trade of the centrally-planned economies, amounted to $ 211 billion in 1968, with the developing countries accounting for $ 43 billion, or 20 per cent of the total. The share of the developing countries has declined from nearly one-third of world exports in 1950 to 20 per cent in 1968.

Two or three factors responsible for this trend may be mentioned here. The world commodity markets, with some exceptions, have exhibited certain unfavourable characteristics. First, their absorptive capacity has grown only slowly, so that increased sales have often been possible only at falling prices. Secondly, these markets have been subject to particularly wide price fluctuations. Thirdly, world trade in primary products, particularly in agricultural products, has been subjected to restrictive practices by industrial countries with a view to providing protection to their own primary producers.[5]

Yet, if dependence on aid is to be reduced, it is imperative that the share of the developing countries in world trade should go on increasing rapidly.

It is against this broader background that the recommendations of the Commission have to be examined. The most important recommendation on the volume of aid may be considered first. The Commission proceeds on the assumption that, the target of aid can be as adequately based on the criterion of 'the ability to pay' of the developed countries as on 'the capital requirements' of the developing countries. The Commission recommends that each developed country should increase its resource transfers to developing countries 'to a minimum of 1 per cent of its GNP as rapidly as possible and in no case later than 1975'. In terms of absolute amounts, this target will mean that the total flow of resources from DAC countries should rise from $ 12.8 billion in 1968 to about $ 23 billion in 1975, or a rise of nearly 80 per cent.

Volume and Mix of Aid

In proposing the 1 per cent target, the Commission is treading on familiar ground. It may be recalled that the United Nations General Assembly had adopted as early as in 1960, a resolution recommending one per cent of the national income as aid. In fact, during some years in the 1960s, the total resource flows did actually exceed one per cent of the

5. World Bank (1969). *Annual Report*.

combined national income of the DAC countries. Hence, there is nothing novel about this target. Perhaps one reason why the Commission thought of reverting to the 1 per cent target nevertheless, is that the performance of some of the developed countries has been rather disappointing in recent years. For instance, in 1968, the percentages of resource flows in respect of the US, the UK and Canada, work out to 0.65, 0.83 and 0.49 respectively. Lurking in the minds of the members of the Commission there might be apprehension that anything a little more ambitious might not evoke the desired response from the developed countries.

The Commission has broken new ground with its recommendation on "aid-mix". In discussions on flow of resources from the developed countries to the developing countries, it must be remembered that not all of this flow is aid. The flow has three main components: official development assistance which could be described as aid proper; secondly, other official flows which might comprise official export credits, etc. and thirdly, private flows including direct and portfolio investments, private export credits, etc. Since the flow of private capital is generally activated by profitability considerations, it does not necessarily flow to priority sectors; nor is private capital always provided on concessional terms. Further, the continuity of the private flow cannot be assumed.

For these reasons, official development assistance remains preferable to private flow. Appreciating this aspect, the Commission has recommended that the commitments of official development assistance should "reach 0.70 per cent of the GNP by 1975 or shortly thereafter, but in no case later than 1980". This target must be compared with the average flow of 0.39 per cent in 1968. If this target is met by 1975, the total quantum of official assistance would reach a level of $ 16.2 billion (in terms of 1968 prices), as compared with a mere $ 6.4 billion in 1968. From the point of view of the developing countries, therefore, this may be regarded as one of the most beneficial recommendations of the commission.

Effectiveness of Aid

Part of the scepticism about aid arises from the suspicion harboured by the donor countries that aid is very often wasted and makes little impact in terms of economic and social development of the recipient countries. The Commission has done signal service to the recipient countries by categorically clearing the air of suspicion. "It is not our impression", the Commission points out, "from the evidence we received, that an excessive amount of aid has been dissipated through abnormal waste, mismanagement, or corruption" (emphasis supplied). On the positive side, the performance of the developing countries during the 1960s is encouraging, with the GNP showing an average rate of increase of 5 per cent per annum. This represents, by any historical standard of comparison, a remarkable rate of growth. These two conclusions of the Commission should silence those critics who would like to give aid a bad name by picking on isolated instances of misapplied aid. Foreign aid, one hopes, will henceforth become more respectable.[6]

Encouraged by past performance, the Commission proposes, that the target for the 1970s should be to raise the annual rate of growth of the GNP in the developing countries to at least 6 per cent, from the current average of 5 per cent. The Commission believes that such an acceleration is clearly feasible for many countries. However, it would have been interesting had the Commission made an attempt to correlate the higher level of aid recommended with the proposed rate of growth.

On the whole, one gets the impression that the Report of the Commission, in trying to be comprehensive in its coverage of problems connected directly or indirectly with aid, becomes discursive in its analysis—somewhat like a Ph.D. dissertation. Thus, its very comprehensiveness becomes a source of weakness. The other recommendations pertain to: trade policies of developed countries, the creation of a favourable climate in developing countries for the flow of foreign private investment, how debt relief should be recognised as a legitimate form of aid, tied and untied aid, food aid, aid administration, IDA replenishment, technical assistance, population planning, aid to education and research and so on. If one looks closely, one can find in the Report, a reference to almost anything of some relevance to aid, as for instance, the "Bisque Clause" incorporated in the post-War loans. Amidst this plethora of recommendations, one finds it almost difficult to distinguish between the central theme, to which overwhelming importance needs to be attached, and the peripheral subjects which might have been as well left to the operative agencies for consideration. Annexure I, on 'The Development Situation', which covers 123 pages and which, though useful, could have been omitted without detracting from the value of the Report. Inadequate fresh thinking on the main theme perhaps stems partly from this obsession with comprehensiveness.

6. Interestingly enough, the *New Statesman* entitled its editorial, discussing the Pearson Commission Report, "Aid is a Three Letter Word", October 3, 1969.

In keeping with the traditional habit of Commissions of breeding Commissions or conferences, the Report has recommended two major conferences. First, it is suggested that the World Bank should convene, in 1970, with a view to coordinating the efforts of aid-givers and recipients, a conference of the appropriate organs of the United Nations, multilateral agencies, representatives of bilateral aid-givers, and the developing countries. This conference could consider the creation of machinery essential to the efficiency and coordination of the international aid system. Second, the DAC should sponsor a meeting of major aid-givers and recipients in 1970, with a view to simplifying procedural obstacles to effective aid implementation. One fails to understand why the Commission itself could not have tackled these problems, at least in broad outlines; the operative part could then have been left to the agencies concerned.

Expectations Belied

The appointment of such a high-powered Commission had given rise to high hopes among the developing countries. Inadequate fresh thinking on crucial issues has resulted in the production of a Report which treads familiar ground. Multilateralisation of aid and the introduction of an element of automaticity in the international aid system are two aspects which, though referred to in the Report, could have done with greater attention. The simplest answer to the question of why developed countries should aid the developing countries is, as the Commission has emphasised, a *moral* one. Since aid does not bless both the giver and the recipient, at any rate in the short run, the relation between the two becomes one of the partnership of unequals. This is hard reality, with which the developing nations have learnt to live. Any proposal which strengthens the weaker partner would tend to promote a better partnership. For instance, if aid to the extent of 1 per cent of GNP were to be elevated to the status of a 'voluntary development tax' to be paid by the developed countries to, say, the IDA, both automacity and multilateralisation might be ensured.

Again, as regards trade policies of the developed countries, it is all very well to recommend the abolition of import duties and excessive excise tax, etc. on primary commodities. Even the massive efforts of the UN Conference on Trade and Development have so far produced little visible results, however. Instead, if the Commission had recommended a

7. Even the title of the Report is reminiscent of "Partners in Progress" issued in 1951 by the US International Development Advisory Board.

compensatory tax, based on the degree of deterioration of terms of trade of developing countries, to be paid voluntarily to IDA by the developed countries an automatic aid replenishment mechanism might perhaps have come into existence. The two instances are cited merely to demonstrate how fundamental rethinking on aid is called for.

Or, take the question of Special Drawing Rights. The Commission is content with merely making this statement on the subject: "The implementation of the agreement to create Special Drawing Rights should serve to lessen the balance of payments problems of some donors and may help to provide an opportunity for a collective attack on the (aid) tying problem". It is regrettable that the question of tilting the creation of Special Drawing Rights in favour of the developing countries did not attract the attention of the Commission. Many Governors of the Fund from the developing countries who spoke at the Annual Meeting reiterated the need to link, in some way, the creation of Special Drawing Rights with aid to developing countries. How exactly such a link could be forged, and to what extent such linking is feasible, are no doubt matters which need detailed consideration. In any case, the fact that the Commission did not consider this aspect at all, is a serious omission indeed.

If the Commission has not succeeded in giving a new direction to aid, what then is the impact that the Report is likely to have on the inflow of aid to developing countries? The major contribution of the Report is that it has expertly clarified the areas of doubt about the value and effectiveness of aid. This should strengthen the hands of the well-intentioned who would like to facilitate the flow of a larger volume of aid. The second important contribution lies in the Commission's emphasis on the relative increase in official development assistance on concessional terms, that is, in the form of grants or loans on soft terms.

The hardening of attitudes towards aid, among the developed countries had recently jeopardised development plans of at least some developing countries. The smooth flow of aid, one hopes, would be resumed as a consequence of the Report. The Chairman of the Commission, however, was more modest while presenting the Report to the Annual Meeting of the World Bank on October 1, 1969: "Indeed, as one who has been exposed for many years to the earthly realities of politics and government, I know that the road to nowhere is paved with good reports...I hope that ours may deserve a better fate. But that will be up to governments. They dispose of what commissions propose."

Part III

Banking and Finance

11

The Rising Rupee and the Forex Reserves

The Rupee has continued to appreciate against the US Dollar. On the basis of monthly average exchange rates, the Rupee appreciated by 2.3 per cent in 2002-03. The Rupee gained further strength during the current financial year: the appreciation during the first four months was around 3 per cent. The Reserve Bank of India's (RBI) reference rate which was Rs. 47.7 per US dollar in mid-March 2003 declined to Rs. 45.22 in mid-March 2004. Some Indian industries which have not grown out of the subsidy syndrome to which they were accustomed to all these years, have begun to complain that such persistent appreciation of the Rupee would adversely affect exports, rendering Indian exports less competitive internationally. To what extent such apprehensions are justified?

Simultaneously, the country's foreign exchange reserves have shown a phenomenal growth with the accretion of about $ 20 billion in 2002-03, the highest accretion in any single year so far: this was the result of the current account surplus on balance of payments, inflows in the form of foreign investment, banking capital and non-resident deposits. This buoyancy in the growth of reserves continued in 2003-04, the reserves soaring to an unprecedented level of nearly $ 110 billion in March 2004, these are equivalent to about two years' import requirements of the country.

Are these two phenomenon unrelated? It is necessary to take a holistic view of developments in the external sector to be able to appreciate the rising Rupee. Indian industries have been able to cast off the crutches of protection as a result of the process of liberalisation and globalisation of the Indian economy. They should regard that learning to live with a floating exchange rate regime forms part of the process of liberalisation and globalisation of the Indian economy. Viewed against this broader perspective, the appreciation of the Rupee becomes a non-issue. It is gratifying to note that some industries like pharmaceuticals have openly expressed confidence in their ability to cope with the rising Rupee. In terms of macroeconomic management, the article seeks to underline, that policy-makers should shift their focus from purely exchange rate management to the issue of productive utilisation of the huge foreign exchange reserves which the economy has unwillingly accumulated.

The world has moved away from the IMF theology of yesteryears of fixed exchange rate regime which stipulated, what is now called 'impossible trinity'—the simultaneous pursuit of a fixed exchange rate, a national monetary policy to contain inflation, and free capital mobility. In fact, it is now recognised that there is no single exchange rate regime which is most appropriate for all countries. For emerging countries like India, Morris Goldstein recommends a 'floating-plus' arrangement which involves a lightly managed float combined with inflation targeting.[1] India has been following this sort of a regime which is guided by the following objectives: reducing excess volatility in exchange rates, preventing the emergence of destabilising speculative activities, helping maintain adequate level of reserves, and developing an orderly foreign exchange market. Intervention by the RBI under such a regime, is not thus, governed by a predetermined target on band around the exchange rate. Containing the impact of the pass-through effect of exchange rate on domestic inflation also forms an important ingredient of such a regime. More recent experience has shown that RBI has succeeded remarkably well in achieving these objectives. Asian currency crisis did not impact on India. Inflation has been contained within a 5 per cent level: and forex reserves, as mentioned above, have been accumulated up to an embarrassingly high level. Overall, the empirical experience shows that exchange rate management has been consistent with macroeconomic stability. This is a remarkable achievement on the part of RBI.

Reverting to the current appreciation of the Rupee, it is important to stress that we should not be led by changes in nominal exchange rates, e.g. exchange rate of the Rupee with the US dollar, to which we have referred to above. The really relevant indicator is what is called real effective exchange rate (REER): that is nominal exchange rate adjusted for relative inflation rates. Again, US is not the only trading partner of India; several other countries are involved, the exchange rates of which also become relevant. RBI publishes regularly the monthly indices of REER

---

1. Patnaik, R.K. (2003). "Exchange Rate Policy and Management: The Indian Experience", *Economic & Political Weekly*, May 31, 2003.

with reference to 31 countries and the Euro area. These data clearly demonstrate that changes in REER are nominal and not substantial. For many months such changes were fractional.[2] Two conclusions can be drawn from these data: first, there are no violent fluctuations in exchange rates; and second, taken as a whole the appreciation of the Rupee is minimal, and not substantial.

That perhaps explains why despite the appreciation of the Rupee against the US dollar, exports have continued to remain buoyant: export growth was 19 per cent in 2002-03 and the growth during the current financial year (up to February 2004) is 14 per cent. Exports getting adversely affected by the appreciation of the Rupee is thus, a myth perhaps created by interest groups.

This brings us to another crucial issue that the exchange rate is important but it is only one of the several factors influencing export growth. For instance, strategic export promotion policies are being designed to guide an export effort, aimed at broadening the coverage to a large number of non-traditional items and markets. The Medium-Term Export strategy announced by the Government in January 2002 involves a comprehensive plan taking into account the contemporary global scenario, to achieve a quantum increase in exports in the medium-term coinciding with the Tenth Plan period (2002-2007). The introduction of a comprehensive system to make tax rebates to exporters transparent and comprehensive, upgradation of export infrastructure, trading agreements, improved access to bank credit and marketing infrastructure, are the other elements of the medium-term strategy of export policy. In fact, it is the technology intensive items that will provide the thrust to such export drive.[3]

In terms of exports prospects therefore, a mildly appreciating Rupee is a non-issue. In fact the cost of imports, of capital goods, or raw materials, would tend to decline in Rupee terms. Industrialists and exporters should, therefore grow out of the subsidy syndrome.

While the track record of RBI in terms of managing the exchange rate is so excellent, in the area of management of the country's foreign exchange reserves it has displayed its total ineptitude. RBI seems to have become a prisoner of its own monumental inertia. First, in terms of the total quantum of reserves. There is, of course, no set formula for

---

2. *RBI Bulletin*, March 2004, p. 255.

3. Reserve Bank of India (2003). *Annual Report*, 2002-03.

determining the optimum level of foreign exchange reserves for a country. There is a threshold level for each country, beyond which the reserves maintained could be characterised as unproductive. Even if we take a liberal view, let us maintain some $ 60 billion of reserves, that is, equivalent to one year's imports beyond which the reserves would be unproductive. This is especially true today when the average interest we earn on investments of our reserves, either in the US or UK would be minimum at say 1 or 2 per cent. There is no reason why we cannot utilise part of our reserves in say importing power plants. Availability of power is acting as a constraint in industrial growth and hence, utilisation of reserves, for import of power plants would confer great benefits to the economy. Second, external commercial borrowings (ECBs) of Corporate Sector. At a time when RBI is flushed with foreign exchange we are permitting corporate sector entities, even some public sector entities, to access foreign funds through borrowing abroad. This is the height of absurdity. While we are earning only 2 or 3 per cent of interest on our reserves, the corporate sector has to pay at least 6 or 7 per cent of interest on such borrowings. Of course, it is conceded that RBI cannot lend directly to private corporate sector; but it is not beyond the ingenuity of RBI to devise a mechanism to facilitate such borrowings. RBI could lend the foreign exchange to public sector banks (PSBs), which can not lend to private sector. Third, no longer is there the *rationale* for continuation of FCNR (foreign currency non-resident) deposits, of the convertible category. We should reduce our dollar liabilities. Those NRIs keen to invest in India could do so in non-convertible Rupee deposits. Fourth, RBI, embarrassed by the high level of reserves seems to be liberalising outward remittances with reckless abandon. Otherwise, what is the *rationale* for permitting Indian nationals to invest abroad to the extent of $ 25,000? We are crying hoarse that the country needs foreign investment funds of a large magnitude on the one hand; and allowing foreign exchange reserves to be frittering away through private investments on the other. Returns to private investment abroad are far from encouraging. Such frittering away of reserves by RBI is reminiscent of the frittering away of the huge sterling balances in the post-War period.

The main thrust of RBI's policy should, therefore, be on how best the country could utilise the huge foreign exchange reserves accumulated over the last couple of years.

12

Two Faces of Banking Sector Reforms

Tracing the course that banking sector reforms in India have taken during the last 15 years between 1990-2005 is an interesting exercise. Over these years, reforms have acquired, as it were, two distinct faces: one which may be broadly categorised as the Basel face, and the other, the Indian face. While the Basel face is the most visible, only the contours of the Indian face are beginning to emerge in the last couple of years. The Basel face refers to the almost mechanistic implementation of Basel norms devised by the Bank for International Settlements (BIS) with the objective of upgrading the Indian banking system to international standards. The Indian face represents a response to India-specific problems, in the solution of which it would be naive to seek solutions in the BIS framework. It is tempting to contemplate whether the emergence of the Indian face could be interpreted as reforms having completed the full cycle, from directed credit to non-directed credit, and back to directed credit. Or, does it signify that Indian policymakers have at last grown up to shed the shibboleths of IMF/World Bank?

The configuration of circumstances when the economy is in the third year of the Tenth Plan (2002-2007) is such that priority sectors would continue to play a critical role in India's future growth and development. Output growth, employment expansion and poverty reduction—all these could be[1] achieved by broad-based and decentralised growth—a phenomenon which needs to be promoted by financial support from the banking system. Viewed from this perspective, the Indian face of banking sector reforms becomes as important as the Basel face.

The Basel Face

In the 1990s, the endeavour of the Indian policymakers was to

---

1. Mujumdar, N.A. (2004). "Role and Relevance of Priority Sector Lending in a Globalised Banking Scenario", *The Journal of Indian Institute of Banking and Finance*, October-December.

benchmark the services of the Indian banking system against "international best practices and standards". This objective was sought to be achieved by implementing the Basel I norms. For instance, the minimum Capital to Risk Assets Ratio (CRAR) has been set at 9 per cent, that is one point above the international norms. The actual CRAR now stands at 12 per cent. Similarly, the risk management models evolved by the BIS have been sought to be transplanted on to the Indian Banking System. What one finds in this whole exercise is the mindless mimicking of Basel models. There is little evidence of suitable country-specific adaptation. The RBI has issued to banks massive tomes on risk management, regurgitating the risk models and other related material liberally listed out by the BIS. One wonders how many public sector bankers really understand these models. Banks are now poised to implement Basel II norms from March 2007 and this would require more capital due to the fact that operational risk is not captured under Basel I.

One of the major objectives of banking sector reforms was to enhance efficiency and productivity of banks through competition. The administered structure of interest rates was dismantled and the level of pre-emption of resources for reserve requirement was reduced. For instance, the Statutory Liquidity Ratio (SLR) for banks was reduced from some 38 per cent to 25 per cent of net demand and the time of liabilities (DTL). New banks were allowed to be established in the private sector and the conditionalities of entry of foreign banks were liberalised. Since 1993, 12 new private sector banks came into existence. Foreign Direct Investment (FDI) in private sector is now allowed up to 74 per cent, subject to the guidelines issued by the Reserve Bank of India (RBI).

What has been the overall impact of these reforms on the banking system? We can do no better than quote Dr. Y.V. Reddy, Governor, RBI: "These reform measures have had major impact on the overall efficiency and stability of the banking system in India."[2] As mentioned above, the capital adequacy of banks is at the international level. The percentage of gross non-performing assets (NPAs) to gross advances has declined from 14.4 per cent in 1998 to 7.2 per cent in 2004. During the last five years the business per employee for public sector banks doubled more than to around Rs. 25 million in 2004. So far so good.

Riding on this euphoria of upgradation of banking services, some policymakers are dreaming of evolving 'giant size' banks by consolidation;

2. Reddy, Y.V. (2005). "Banking Sector Reforms in India: An Overview", *Reserve Bank of India Bulletin*, June.

and of making such banks 'globally competitive'. It is a moot point whether efficiency in banking is size-neutral or whether there are indeed economics of scale. Nor is it clear whether evolving globally competitive banks deserves to be placed on the top of the agenda of banking reforms, at this stage of India's development. Our submission is that there are some neglected areas in domestic banking, which need to be addressed immediately. This brings us to the Indian face of banking reforms.

Untold Story

Before we take up the discussion of the Indian face of banking reforms, there is an untold story of reforms—untold in the sense of not being recorded in official chronicles of RBI or IMF/World Bank—which needs to be highlighted here. One of the by-products of banking reforms was the deceleration in the quantum of flow of credit to the rural sector, and the deterioration of the health of the rural credit delivery system as a whole. The interest rate regime which appeared to be designed to pamper private corporate sector openly discriminated against the agricultural sector. In fact banking reforms, or financial sector reforms generally, were inspired by the market theology of IMF/World Bank. The Narasimham Committee which in effect packaged this theology in the Indian bottle was bold enough to recommend that the target for priority sector credit should be reduced to 10 per cent from the then prevailing target of 40 per cent of net bank credit.[3] Does not market theology stipulate that directed credit should be shunned? Interest rates should be risk-related and interest rate subsidies eliminated. Of course, good sense prevailed and RBI did not formally reduce the target. But it appeared that both RBI and PSBs generally supported Narasimham Committee's recommendation in spirit. This had disastrous consequences for agricultural growth.

For most of the years in the 1990s, PSBs merrily defaulted on the credit targets of 18 per cent of net bank credit to agriculture and 40 per cent of net credit of priority sectors.[4] The RBI, which was obsessively preoccupied with the implementation of Basel norms, winked at the defaults. While the priority sector target has been attained during the last couple of years, the target for agriculture continues to remain unattained. In the milieu of the new banking culture fostered by reforms, lending to

---

3. Narasimham, M. (1991). *Report of the Committee on Financial System*, Reserve Bank of India, Mumbai; and *Report of the Committee on Banking Reforms*, Reserve Bank of India, Mumbai, 1998.
4. Shetty, S.L. (2004). "Distributional Issues in Bank Credit", *Economic and Political Weekly*, July 17.

agriculture or priority sectors generally became unfashionable. The focus of PSBs shifted to the three "Cs"—namely corporate elite, consumer credit and capital market related activities.

While highly rated corporate entities could raise money from banks or PSBs at interest rates as low as 6 or 7 per cent, the small farmer was required to pay a rate of 12 per cent. According to market theology, subsidies should be shunned. It was left to the Government of India to reduce the lending rate to small farmer to 8 per cent only in August 2003. RBI's neglect of agriculture and the rural sector generally in the 1990s was total: it failed to arrest the deterioration of the health of all institutions involved in rural credit: PSBs, cooperative credit institutions and RRBs—all of which showed high NPAs. In other words, a by-product of implementing mindlessly Basel norms was that the rural credit delivery system became sick and the agricultural sector suffered. Dr. Manmohan Singh, the Prime Minister admits: "what is alarming, however, is that there seems to have been a neglect of agriculture in the past decade."[5] No wonder the average annual growth rate of agriculture decelerated sharply, to lower than 2 per cent. If we have to ensure a sustained growth of GDP of 7 or 8 per cent in the coming years, agricultural growth will have to be stepped to say 4 per cent. The Tenth Plan assumes such a growth rate; but in reality, the average growth rate for first three years of the Tenth Plan was hardly 1.5 per cent.

The unkindest cut of all was the disenfranchisement of small farmers. There was a dramatic decline in the number of small borrowal accounts with credit limit of Rs. 25,000: their number which had reached 62.55 million in March 1992 dipped to only 36.87 million by March 2003. The credit outstanding of this category of accounts which formed nearly 22 per cent of total outstanding credit in 1992 dipped to only 5.4 per cent in 2003. Were PSBs trying to boost their profits by economics of 'exclusion'?

I have documented extensively elsewhere, how the reforms fad led to the total neglect of rural credit and sickness of the rural credit delivery system, as a whole.[6]

---

5. Singh, Manmohan (2005). "Second Green Revolution in Indian Agriculture", Address at the Agriculture Summit 2005, *Economic Developments in India*, Vol. 89, Academic Foundation, New Delhi.

6. Mujumdar, N.A. (2002). *Financial Sector Reforms and India's Economic Development*, Vol. 1 & 2, Academic Foundation, New Delhi; and also Mujumdar, N.A. (2004). *Economic Reforms Sans Development*, Academic Foundation, New Delhi.

The Indian Face

The rather belated recognition of the damage that banking sector reforms had inflicted on the rural sector has led the Government of India to take policy decisions in the following three areas: Enlarging the flow of credit to agriculture, and to small industries and rebuilding the cooperative credit structure. These initiatives are in a way a response to the 'untold story' referred to above. The contours of the Indian face of the banking reforms have, thus, begun to emerge.

First, the new Common Minimum Programme (NCMP) announced by the UPA Government in 2004 stipulates that bank credit to agriculture be doubled in the next three years. PSBs have applied themselves seriously to attaining this target. In the first year itself, credit to agriculture has been stepped up by some 30 per cent. This is indeed, a welcome development.

Second, the policy package announced by the Ministry of Finance, Government of India, in August 2005, for small and medium enterprises (SMEs) stipulates that credit to SMEs should be doubled in the next five years: from Rs. 67,000 crore in 2004-05 to Rs. 1,35,000 crore in 2009-10. That is, PSBs should achieve a 20 per cent year-on-year expansion on credit to this sector.[7]

Third, about the rebuilding of the cooperative credit institutions. The Government of India constituted in August 2004, a Task Force, under the Chairmanship of Prof. A. Vaidyanathan to formulate a practical and implementable plan of action and also assess the broad dimensions of the financial assistance that Government of India will have to extend to rejuvenate the rural cooperative credit structure. In its Report submitted in February 2005, the Task Force has placed the overall financial assistance required at Rs. 10,839 crore and an additional Rs. 4,000 crore towards contingencies, needs to be provided. NABARD has been designated as the Nodal Agency to coordinate the implementation of the entire programme.[8] This relates to short-term credit. The Task Force is now engaged in recommending measures to revive the long-term cooperative credit structure.

While on this subject it is necessary to refer to another subtle reform that is taking place in the rural credit delivery system, namely, micro-finance. The programme of linking SHGs with the banking system has

7. *Economic and Political Weekly*, August 20, 2005.

8. NABARD, *Annual Report, 2004-05*.

emerged as the major micro-finance programme. The RBI has been seeking to create an appropriate environment for the nurturing of non-governmental organisations engaged in micro-finance activities. Banks are being encouraged to adopt the agency model by using the infrastructure of civil society organisations, rural kiosks and village knowledge centres for providing credit support to farm or rural sector generally.[9]

Analytically, it is interesting to note that initiatives in this area have come mainly from Government of India (GoI) and not RBI. It is as if the GoI is telling the RBI: you focus on the Basel face and we will take care of the Indian face.

World Bank's Assessment

In sharp contrast to Dr. Reddy's highly analytical assessment of banking reforms, referred to above, the World Bank's assessment appears to be amateurish, doctrinaire and bereft of any insights into realities of contemporary banking issues. In 2002, the World Bank had organised a Conference on India's financial sector.[10] Obsession to pamper the private corporate sector and a congenital dislike of the public sector are writ large on these papers. At the same time, the World Bank is keen to demonstrate its synergy with the Government of India's recent changes in policy stance regarding poverty and the small man. It, therefore, makes appropriate noises. This leads to some degree of ambivalence in the Bank's affirmations. For instance, take the following paragraph from the Foreword to the book, mentioned above, by Mr. Michael F. Carter, Country Director, India, World Bank:

> "These reforms have helped improve soundness and depth of the financial sector and led to an impressive growth in the country's financial resources. But much more needs to be done to ensure the efficient allocation of these resources to finance the higher levels of investment necessary for sustained growth and poverty reduction. The private sector has not received credit at the expected levels. And large segments of the economy such as small and medium enterprises and rural households remain excluded from access to formal finance" (emphasis supplied).

Has the World Bank discovered in 2005 that one of the objectives of bank credit is to reduce poverty? Its crocodile tears for SMEs and rural

9. Reserve Bank of India (2005). *Annual Report, 2004-05.*
10. Papers presented at the Conference have been published in a book entitled: *India's Financial Sector: Recent Reforms, Future Challenges*, Priya Basu (ed.), Macmillan, New Delhi, 2005.

households are equally inconsistent with the reforms designed within the framework of market theology. Both the IMF and World Bank monitor the Indian economy on a continuing basis. Why did they not advise the Government of India or RBI that the mindless implementation of the Basel norms and associated risk management models of BIS is proving anti-poor and hence, mid-course policy correctives need to be introduced? Far from extending the reach of formal finance, as we have seen, one of the by-products of reforms has been to throw out, a large number of small farmers, of the ambit of formal finance.

Again, the World Bank has been always a patron of the private sector, particularly private corporate sector. But to argue that 'it has not received the credit at the expected levels', is factually incorrect. In fact, the private corporate sector never had it so good. The soft interest rate regime was specially designed for it. In terms of quantum of credit, there was actually a surfeit of credit, especially for the high rated corporate entities. The external commercial borrowings (ECBs) soared to $ 11.5 billion in 2004-2005. It is common knowledge that the private corporate sector was highly liquid in recent years because of the massive inflows of resources. Some corporates made money by investing their surplus resources in short-term monetary instruments. All this, is well documented. One would wish that the World Bank experts update themselves with the recent developments, before making such sweeping statements. If anything, it was the rural sector which was crowded out.

Take one more sample from the Foreword: "Equally, there is a need to deal with the country's public sector banks and financial institutions: there are good reasons to doubt whether government control can be made consistent with the efficiency and commercialisation of these institutions". Is private management and control the paragon of efficiency? The issue has acquired a contemporary relevance with the recent fall from grace of the American capitalist image. Revelations of corporate crookedness and accounting scandals have shaken the very foundations of the American Capitalist model. The London Economist sums up the situation: 'Chief executives and accountants have become a dispised breed, less trusted than even politicians and journalists'.[11] Essentially, efficiency is ownership neutral. One could, of course, discuss providing operational autonomy to PSBs but that is a different matter.

11. *The Economist*, November 30, 2002.

One final sample. Priya Basu, Lead Specialist, Finance and Private Sector for India, at the World Bank writes:

"Banking system distress in India is considerable both in absolute terms and when compared with distress faced by many of the East Asian countries on the eve of their crisis. Much of India's banking system is affected by a weak credit culture, poor risk assessment and management, supervision and regulation that is not fully in line with international standards and an inefficient legal and judicial framework"(p. 108).

This is indeed alarming. If only Priya Basu had done some homework and traced the more recent policy measures taken, including in the area of supervision and risk management, as spelt out by Dr. Reddy, she would have realised that her apprehensions regarding the Indian banking system are ill-founded.

Governance Dividend

While on this subject, it can be recalled here that only a few years ago a team of three financial wizards, set up by Indian Merchants Chamber had examined the PSBs and had recommended that the four weak banks, which were beyond redemption, be closed. In retrospect, it looks how presumptuous the recommendation was. All these banks have turned the corner and are in pretty good shape today. Such premature judgements do more harm to the banking system, than good. All these banks have derived 'Governance Dividend', from good governance. To rejuvenate a bank, it is not enough to inject additional capital but it is necessary to upgrade governance also.

In this context we need to ponder over, Dr. Reddy's prophetic pronouncement, which has not received the attention it deserves, "Consolidation, competition, and risk management are no doubt critical to the future of banking but I believe that governance and financial inclusion would also emerge as key issues for a country like India, at this stage of socio-economic development." The Indian face of banking reforms is all about 'inclusion'. In the coming years, the focus will have to be also on governance. This holds true as much for the cooperative credit sector as for the commercial banks. Perhaps a measure of operational autonomy to PSBs should form an ingredient of good governance.

Reforms Counter–Productive?

Has there been a reversal, as it were, of market theology-led reforms? Three areas can be briefly discussed: directed credit, reserve requirements and capital market. First, we have realised that directed credit is necessary to ensure that the end-objectives of growth with equity are achieved. Our brief experiment with giving full freedom to banks in the area of deployment of credit, *alas*, proved counter-productive. Second, in terms of reserve requirements, reforms sought to reduce the high-levels of pre-emption of bank resources in the form of reserve requirements. The Narasimham Committee had recommended, for instance, that the statutory reserve ratio (SRR) be reduced to 25 per cent of net demand and time liabilities (DTL) and this recommendation was implemented. But what has happened in practice? The investment-deposit ratio of banks has continued to remain, for most of the years, in the region of 38 to 40 per cent of DTL. In other words, banks have continued to invest in government securities a substantially larger proportion of their resources, than what is prescribed. For instance, commercial banks excess holdings of SLR securities—excess in the sense of higher than the prescribed ratio—added to a staggering figure of Rs. 2,24,701 crore at end-September 2005.[12] This has serious implications for utilisation of banks resources. Massive resources of this order are being weaned away from supporting productive sectors of the economy to support Government consumption: consumption, because the central Government incurs a deficit on revenue account. Apart from crowding out productive sectors, it also promotes fiscal profligacy. Is this evidence of reforms bringing about more efficient allocation of resources? The reform has proved counter-productive. Neither the IMF nor the World Bank has pointed out this aberration. I have argued that RBI should fix, along with the minimum SLR of 25 per cent, a maximum of say 30 per cent. Only thus, could we facilitate flow of larger resources to support productive sectors of the economy. Third, following the IMF/World Bank theology, development of the capital market has been almost an obsession of the governments in the 1990s as also at present. Various artificial props like throwing open the portfolio investment to Foreign Institutional Investors (FIIs), asking PSBs to increase their exposure to the capital market, both directly and indirectly, and exemption of dividends from income-tax have been given. Capital market is supposed to promote a more efficient allocation of investible resources. What is the net result? The Sensex may have risen to new heights but what about the quantum of resources we are able to raise? In 2004-05, resource mobilisation from the primary market through public

12. Reddy, Y.V. (2005). *Mid-Term Review of Annual Policy Statement for the Year 2005-06*, October 25, 2005, p. 11.

issues added up to only Rs. 21,900 crore. In sharp contrast, mobilisation of resources through private placement was around to Rs. 84,100 crore. Have the efforts to develop the capital market proved counter-productive? What happens to the more efficient allocation of investible resources through the market? These are issues to be pondered over.

Conclusion

Finally, it should be recognised that the dichotomy, created during the reforms phase, between the Basel face and the Indian face is artificial, extending financial support to broad-based decentralised growth is as much a responsibility of the banking system as financing private corporate sector. The two faces should be regarded as profiles of a single face. Both these aspects of banking should be mutually supportive and complementary to each other. Dr. Y.V. Reddy, Governor, RBI shows a rare insight into this complex issue when he sums up the situation admirably in the following statement made recently, "...we in India have to focus on extending financial services in both rural and urban areas for ensuring financial inclusion of all segments of the population. At the same time, one should avoid the temptation of creating one set of banking and financial institutions to cater to the poor or the unorganised, and another for the rest. The medium to long-term objective should be to ensure inclusion of all segments in the mainstream institutions, while taking advantage of the flexibility of multiplicity of models of delivering a wide range of financial services. In this light a comprehensive framework to revive cooperative credit system, revitalise RRBs and reorient commercial banking system needs to get a high priority while simultaneously encouraging and enabling the growth of micro-finance movement in India, which has been very successful".[13]

---

13. Reddy, Y.V. (2005). Address at the Micro-Finance Conference organised by the Indian School of Business, Hyderabad, August 6.

13

Monetary Policy: January 2006

Containing Inflationary Forces

The Governor of the Reserve Bank of India (RBI), Dr. Y.V. Reddy, released, on January 24, 2006, the 'Third Quarter Review of Annual Statement on Monetary Policy for the Year 2005-06'. There are no major changes in, the monetary measures. For instance, the bank rate remains unchanged at 6 per cent and the cash reserve ratio (CRR) of banks remains unchanged at 5 per cent.

The only changes introduced are in the repo rates:

First, the fixed reverse repo rate under the liquidity adjustment facility (LAF) of RBI has been raised by 25 basis points from 5.25 per cent to 5.50 per cent.

Second, the fixed repo rate under the LAF will be 6.50 per cent. This is because the repo rate will continue to be linked to the reverse repo rate, mentioned above. The spread between reverse repo rate and the repo rate has been retained at 100 basis points, as at present.

Although, these changes appear to be rather nominal, they have triggered the expectation that this is the beginning of an upward rising interest rate structure. Has the low interest rate regime come to an end? Already, some housing finance companies like HDFC and LIC have indicated that they may raise their lending rates. There is also the speculation that deposit rates may be hiked up. The yield on government securities is on the uptrend: for instance, the yield on 10 years bond rose to 7.45 per cent on 25th January from 7.33 per cent on the previous day. Do these developments signal the eventual emergence of a high interest structure? This brief article seeks to show that there are more fundamental macroeconomic factors, which have provoked RBI to take these measures. In fact, an analysis of the underlying factors would show that Dr. Reddy's measures are in the nature of anticipatory action, in the sense that his statement provides penetrating insights into the emerging demand pressures.

The Outlook for Growth

The outlook for growth this year, that is, 2005-06, is very bright. Based on the pick up in agricultural output and the robust performance of industrial and service sectors, GDP is expected to grow at 7.5 to 8 per cent. Perhaps this optimistic outlook explains the runaway expansion of bank credit. Non-food credit increased by 24 per cent during the current year up to January 6, 2006, close on the heels of an expansion of nearly 20 per cent during the previous year. In terms of industry, significant increases were recorded by power, iron and steel, automobiles, chemicals and chemical products, textiles, gems and jewellery, petroleum, coal, etc. In the services sector, the growth in credit was led by housing, commercial real estate, and personal loans. Credit to commercial real estate and personal loans have been rising significantly above the trend rates of growth. Credit to agriculture has been growing at 39 per cent on a year-to-year basis since 2004-05. Against this background, the following paragraphs of the Governor's statement are worth underlining:

"While strong credit growth, which is well diversified, is a reflection of greater credit penetration and investment activity, there are concerns about the credit quality in the expansion phase. The Reserve Bank has already announced some measures and sensitised banks in this regard. Recent trends in credit growth warrant reiteration of these concerns. Banks are urged to undertake a comprehensive review of credit quality, including a segment wise analysis of activities with reference to those sectors where credit is expanding rapidly" (p.31, para 60).

Aggregate deposits of banks rose by 14 per cent during 2005-06 up to January 6, 2006, as compared with an increase of 10 per cent during the corresponding period of the previous year. A characteristic feature of this year's deposits growth is the spurt in demand deposits which rose by a staggering dimension of more than 30 per cent. In contrast, the growth was slightly less than 20 per cent during the previous year. The runaway expansion of bank credit, referred to above, and the unusual spurt in demand deposits perhaps, reflect the potential demand pressures.

Perhaps, the third element in this configuration of demand pressures is that, asset prices in housing, equity and bullion have continued to accelerate. RBI has already initiated some action to contain these pressures. Surveillance over exposure limits in the banking system in respect of sensitive sectors such as equity markets has been stepped up, and risk weights for calculation of capital adequacy have been increased in respect of housing and real estate.

Taking these features of the current economic situation into account, the Governor sounds a note of caution on inflation:

"The risks to inflation from both domestic and global developments remain high persisting well into 2006-07. In particular, the remaining pass-through of international crude prices into domestic prices of LPG and Kerosene for inflation portends an upward bias to inflation in 2006-07" (p.35, para 65).

RBI is committed to take measures in a calibrated and prompt manner to stabilise inflation expectations in response to evolving circumstances and the January 2006 measures should be judged against this perspective. "The overriding importance of monitoring well anchored inflation expectations is critical for sustaining the growth momentum and assuring macroeconomic and financial stability" (p.25, para 54).

Repo Rates and Interest Rate Structure

Finally, a word about how repo rates may affect the general interest rate structure. As we all know, repo (repurchase obligation) is a money market instrument involving two tiers of transactions, between bank and RBI. The term 'repo' refers to purchase of securities by RBI and injection of liquidity in the banking system, while 'reverse repo' refer to sale of securities by RBI and absorption of liquidity. Since November 1997, RBI has been conducting repo transactions on fixed rates. Thus, repo provides a collateralised funding alternative. It must be added that apart from banks, RBI has allowed some mutual funds, housing finance companies, and insurance companies to undertake repo transactions through accounts maintained with custodians.

Thus, when the repo rates rise, the cost of funds to banks rises, and as a consequence banks are expected to raise their own lending rates. What is perhaps more important, the raising of repo rates is taken by banks as a signal by the Central Bank for the upward movement of interest rates in general. Hence, the extent of the rise in repo rates is not as significant as the rise by itself. High lending rates are expected to moderate the runaway expansion of bank credit witnessed this year. Of course, high interest rate is an important, but not the only instrument, for moderating demand pressures. This measure needs to be buttressed by other measurers to rein in demand pressures and thereby, inflationary forces.

14

The Budget for 2006-07 and the Bankers

The Union Budget for 2006-07 presented to the Lok Sabha on February 28, 2006 has provoked a good deal of discussion both in the print and electronic media. But it is necessary to analyse more specific issues relevant to the banking industry: What does the Budget hold for bankers? Do the measures announced in the Budget warrant any changes in the strategy of banking operations? In the light of the assessment of the economy embodied in the Budget, what are the prospects of the banking industry in the medium-term? This brief article seeks to address these and related issues.

Outlook for the Economy

Let us begin with the outlook for the economy. Basically, the growth of bank deposits is a function of national income. According to Central Statistical Organisation's (CSO) advance estimates, national income (GDP) growth is likely to be 8.1 per cent for the current year 2005-06. This is among the highest growth rates recorded by the Indian economy. In fact GDP growth exceeding 8 per cent has been achieved only in five years of recorded history and two of these five are in the last three years. The target for GDP growth for the Tenth Five Year Plan (2002-2007) was set at 8 per cent. Going by the performance of the economy so far, the actual annual average rate of GDP growth would turn out to be 7 per cent. It is no wonder that this record achievement has created an element of euphoria about future growth of the economy. For instance, the Prime Minister was emboldened to state recently that we should be aiming at 10 per cent growth in the coming years. This euphoria about growth prospects is reflected in the capital market: the Sensex rose by 450 points, since the Budget, to reach 10,735 on March 6, 2006.

The outlook for growth of the banking sector in the medium-term are thus, obviously bright. The current year itself reflects the buoyancy of deposits growth: aggregate deposits of scheduled commercial banks rose by more than 14 per cent (Rs. 2,71,890 crore) up to February 3, 2006, as compared to an increase of about 10 per cent (Rs. 1,72,860 crore) in the corresponding period of the previous year. This buoyancy would continue to persist if the growth of the economy is sustained at 7 or 8 per cent in the coming years.

Conversion of Special Securities and Tax Exemption of Fixed Deposits

The Budget has announced two important measures which would go a considerable way to boost banks' resources.

First, the conversion of special securities into tradable securities; and second, making fixed deposits with banks eligible for tax exemption.

It may be recalled that as part of the banking sector reforms introduced in 1993-94, capital was infused in nationalised banks by issue of special securities, of the order of Rs. 16,809 crore. To this figure, if we add perpetual securities issued earlier, the total capital support stands at Rs. 22,808 crore. The Budget now seeks to covert these special securities which are non-tradable into tradable, SLR Government of India Securities. This measure will have the effect of enlarging the total resources of banks for onlending to the productive sectors of the economy. Banks can now treat these securities as part of their SLR Securities, trade in them and park them with Reserve Bank of India through repo transactions. This measure would indeed greatly benefit those nationalised banks which have a large chunk of the special securities.

Regarding fixed deposits, henceforth investments in fixed deposits in scheduled banks for a term of not less than five years would be eligible for tax exemption under Section 80C of the Income Tax Act. It may be recalled that to give boost to the capital market, income from investments in equities and in mutual funds was exempt from income tax but not interest income from fixed deposits with banks. Thus, fiscal policy openly discriminated against banks. To the small investor bank deposits became unattractive not only because of lower deposit rates in the low interest rate regime but also because they did not attract tax concession. At long last, this discrimination has ended. We must realise that commercial banks play as important a role in financing the productive sectors of the economy as the development banks or the capital market. The correction of fiscal discrimination against banks is indeed welcome. Banks should now focus on encouraging customers, to opt for deposits of five years and above, and perhaps also offer attractive deposit rates for this category of deposits. Thus, banks should be able to mobilise larger deposits during the year 2006-07.

Initiatives in Farm Credit

The Budget for 2006-07 is notable for a number of initiatives it has taken in the area of farm or rural credit. These can be briefly discussed under the following four heads: quantum jump in rural credit, concessional lending rates, micro-finance and issue of 'inclusion'.

It may be recalled here that the National Common Minimum Programme (NCMP) had stipulated doubling of farm credit in three years. The performance in both the years 2004-05 and 2005-06 exceeded the targets. The Finance Minister has asked banks to increase the level of credit to Rs. 1,75,000 crore in 2006-07 and also add another 50 lakh farmers to their portfolio. Since tenant farmers are not adequately served, the Finance Minister has asked banks to open a separate window for Self-Help Groups (SHGs) and joint liability groups of tenant farmers to ensure that a certain proportion of total farm credit is extended to this category of farmers as well.

Concessional lending to farmers is sought to be provided by extending subsidies in two ways. First, farmers who have borrowed crop loans from scheduled commercial banks, RRBs and Primary Agricultural Credit Societies (PACs) during 2005-06 will get a relief on their interest liability equal to 2 percentage points, of the total interest-liability. In other words, if they had borrowed at say 9 per cent their interest liability would be reduced to 7 per cent. The required amount would be credited to their bank accounts before March 31, 2006. The Budget makes a provision of Rs. 1,700 crore for this purpose.

Secondly, Government has decided to ensure that farmers receive short- term credit at an interest rate of 7 per cent, with an upper limit, of Rs. 3,00,000 on the principal amount. This would be provided through subsidising NABARD which refinances commercial banks lending to agriculture. This measure would come into effect from the 2006-07 *Kharif* season.

It should be underlined that in both the cases mentioned above, the subvention would be provided by the Government and hence, there will be no burden on the lending banks.

Micro-Finance

Considerable progress has been made in respect of linking SHGs to banks. Today, 801,000 SHGs are linked to banks and the credit disbursed to these SHGs is around Rs. 4,863 crore. The Finance Minister has asked banks to credit-link another 3,85,000 SHGs in 2006-07.

A Bill to provide statutory framework for micro finance sector development would be introduced in this Session of Parliament. Taken together, these initiatives, in a way, set out the agenda of action for public sector banks.

Committee on Financial Inclusion

One of the major concerns of rural credit has been that institutional finance does not reach all the potential borrowers in the rural sector. For instance, the findings of NSS 59th Round (2003) reveal that out of the total number of cultivator households only 27 per cent receive credit from formal sources and 22 per cent from informal sources. The remaining households, mainly small and marginal farmers, virtually remain outside the purview of institutional finance. With a view to bringing such cultivator households within the fold of institutional finance, the Finance Minister has announced his decision to appoint a Committee on Financial Inclusion. The Committee would investigate the causes underlying the exclusion of such farmers and would sketch a blueprint for ensuring that all households seeking credit from lending institutions would be able to access such credit.

It is an irony of financial history that during the 1990s, in the euphoria of banking sector reforms, public sector banks shed a large number of small borrowal accounts. In other words, small farmers who had access to bank credit were thrown out of the banking system. Whatever may have been the reasons, this was unfortunate. The pendulum has swung, now to the other extreme and we are now seeking to bring as many farmers as possible, into the fold of the banking system.

All these budget measures designed to revive the agricultural sector should be seen in the light of the current food security scenario. The Government of India has recently announced that half-a-million tonnes of wheat would be imported 'initially'. This is a clear reflection of the critical food supply situation.

Business Facilitators/Correspondents

Finally, the Budget also refers to appointment of banking correspondents or banking agents. With the objective of extending savings and loan facilities to the under-privileged and unbanked population, the Reserve Bank of India has advised banks to use the services of non-governmental organisations (NGOs)/Self-Help Groups (SHGs), Micro-Finance Institutions (MFIs) and other Civil Society Organisations (CSOs) as intermediaries in providing financial and banking services. These intermediaries could act as business facilitators or correspondents. Commercial banks, do not have to obtain RBI's prior approval for using these intermediaries as business facilitators. The guidelines issued by RBI in this respect are published in RBI's Monetary and Credit Information Review, February 2006. How far this *modus operandi* would be effective in extending the reach of the banking system, time alone can demonstrate.

15

Monetary Policy: April 2006

Forewarning Hardening of Interest Rates

On the face of it, the monetary policy package, announced by the Reserve Bank of India (RBI), Governor Dr. Y.V. Reddy, on April 18, 2006 appears to be designed to maintain the *status quo*.

(i) The Bank Rate remains unchanged at 6 per cent; (ii) The reverse repo rate remains unchanged at 5.5 per cent, and the fixed repo rate will continue to be 6.5 per cent; (iii) The cash reserve ratio (CRR) will continue to remain at 5 per cent; and (iv) The interest rate on savings bank deposits regulated by RBI remains unchanged at 3.5 per cent. However, going by these formal indicators, it should be a mistake to dismiss the announcement as a non-event.

Three Worrying Features

The runaway expansion of credit and the tightening of liquidity in the banking system had led to market expectations that there would be some hardening of interest rates. Non-food credit was the key driver of banking activity, rising by 37.3 per cent in 2005-06, close on the heels of a rise of 27.5 recorded during the previous year. Credit growth outpaced deposit growth by a substantial margin. The year-on-year incremental non-food credit-deposit ratio continued to remain high at 113 per cent during 2005-2006, as compared to 117 per cent a year ago. More importantly, the incremental non-food credit-deposit ratio jumped from 90 per cent in the first half of 2005-06 to 132 per cent in the second half of the year.

There were pressures on the liquidity of the banking system; the redemption of India Millennium Deposits (IMD) at end-December 2005, drained liquidity to the extent of Rs. 32,000 crore. In fact RBI had to inject liquidity during the subsequent period: daily injections of liquidity under the Liquidity Adjustment Facility (LAF) averaged Rs. 11,686 crore during January-March 2006.

Money Supply (M_3) also accelerated to 20.4 per cent in 2005-06, from an increase of 12.1 per cent during the previous year. What is interesting is that despite these three worrying features, namely runaway expansion of bank credit, tighter liquidity and larger expansion in money supply, inflation continued to be contained within a reasonable band inflation measured by variations in the wholesale prices index (WPI), on a year-on-year basis, was 4 per cent at end-March 2006, compared to a peak of 6 per cent reached on April 23, 2005. Perhaps this remarkable performance in the area of management of inflation by RBI provides the key to why Governor Reddy chose not to hike interest rates in his April policy pronouncement.

Forewarning about Inflation

Dr. Reddy's address embodied in the highly analytical 73 page document entitled "Annual Policy Statement for the Year 2006-07" forewarns in unmistakable terms about higher inflation waiting to happen and which would logically lead to hardening of interest rates. In fact this forms the central message of the April monetary policy package.

Containing Inflation

Two distinct aspects of inflation management need to be spelt out in this context. First, inflation potential has been suppressed for the time being but which may manifest itself fully any time in the future. The second element in the configuration of demand pressures is that asset prices in housing, equity and bullion have continued to accelerate. Surveillance over exposure limits of the banking system in respect of sectors such as equity markets, has already been stepped up; and risk weights for calculation of capital adequacy have been increased in respect of housing and real estate. The April measures further reinforce efforts in this direction.

In terms of potential inflation, as a matter of policy, we have not allowed international oil prices to be fully transmitted on to the domestic oil prices. In this context we can do no better than quote the following sentence from Dr. Reddy's statement, "The incomplete pass-through to the prices of domestic petroleum products, particularly kerosene, liquified petroleum gas (LPG), and to a small extent in petrol and diesel, appropriate timing of administered price increases into the retreating phase of inflation during the first half of 2005-06 and some burden sharing by oil companies as well as through customs/excise duty reductions mitigated the immediate cost push impact of international crude prices" (p.10). International oil prices, have continued to rise and one sees little hope of their returning to normal levels. We may thus, be forced to permit their full transmission to domestic prices.

The openness of the Indian economy has also meant that we have to assign more weight to global factors while formulating monetary policy. To quote Dr. Reddy again, "The adverse consequences of further escalation of international crude prices and/or of disruptive unwinding of global imbalances are likely to be pervasive across economies, including India. Moreover, in a situation of generalised tightening of monetary policy, India cannot afford to stay out of step" (page 39). The message is, thus, loud and clear: We are poised to move over to a high interest rate regime.

The other set of measures of increasing general provisioning requirement on standard advances in specific sectors, namely, personal loans, loans and advances qualifying as capital market exposures, residential housing loans beyond Rs. 20 lakh and commercial real estate loans—points to the same direction of upward movement of interest rates. Such provisioning requirement has been raised from the present level of 0.4 per cent to 1 per cent. More recently, property prices in metros and even in smaller towns have shown an alarming rise. To moderate such a rise, RBI has increased the risk weight on bank's exposures to commercial real estate from 125 per cent to 150 per cent. It may be recalled that in July 2005, this risk weight had been raised from 100 per cent to 125 per cent.

Within a fortnight of the credit policy announcement, the higher provisioning requirements have resulted in the hike in lending rates. State Bank of India has hiked interest rates on home loans by 25 basis points with effect from May 1, 2006.

Moreover, the runaway expansion of credit has also driven banks to seek to mobilise larger deposits by offering higher deposit rates. State Bank of India has also raised the deposit rates by 50 basis points. This means the cost of funds to the bank would rise and hence, the SBI has raised the Benchmark. Prime Lending rate by 50 basis points to 10.75 per cent. Perhaps other banks were waiting for the SBI to take the lead and there would be a general rise in interest rates. Major housing finance companies are already contemplating to raise their interest rates on home loans. HDFC has raised interest on home loans by half-a-percentage point and its Prime Lending Rate from 11.25 per cent to 11.75 per cent.

Thus, it is a tribute to the ingenuity of Governor Dr. Reddy that while creating the general impression of maintaining the *status quo*, he has succeeded in achieving his covert objective of moving the banking system to a higher interest rate regime.

16

Credit Policies and Financial Inclusion

The concept of financial inclusion extends far beyond the question of merely bringing all cultivators, including the small and the marginal, into the fold of institutional credit as the current official discourses on the subject seem to suggest. The point is that financial inclusion needs to be contextualised. From the point of view of macroeconomic objectives, it has become necessary to follow, at this stage of India's development, the path of inclusive growth, which essentially means broad-based and decentralised growth. The title of the draft approach paper to the Eleventh Five Year Plan—'Towards Faster and More Inclusive Growth'—itself reflects the recognition of this need. Financial inclusion can be regarded as a counterpart of the inclusive growth in the real sector. Viewed from this broader perspective, this article seeks to demonstrate, that financial inclusion becomes a growth and development imperative: growth, because a high GDP growth rate like the 8 per cent targeted in the Eleventh Plan (2007-2012) can be sustained only if other sectors or segments of the economy, which would be discussed presently, can be activated; development, because this is perhaps the best route by which the bulk of the poor can be provided with livelihood and food security.

Monetary and credit policymakers should, therefore, have a clear vision of the new architecture of the financial institutions which would facilitate broad-based and decentralised growth of the economy. Is there a need for new institutional formations? What should be the interlinkages among these institutions and the kind of support mechanism that needs to be in place to foster some of these institutions in terms subsidies or credit guarantee schemes? These questions pose challenges to both policymakers and development researchers. Managing the changing challenges of inclusive growth in the real sector should make us rethink of the role of different financial institutions involved and their competencies. This broadens the agenda of the credit policymakers.

No doubt some measures are already underway to streamline the cooperative credit structure following the recommendations of the Vaidyanathan Committee. There is also a move towards consolidation of RRBs. The SHGs—Bank linkage programme has emerged as the largest micro-finance programme. Welcome as these efforts are, they appear rather fragmentary and isolated, whereas what is warranted is a holistic approach. This article seeks to explore the possibilities of sketching an integrated picture.

Genesis of Official Discourses

The genesis of the current official discourses on financial inclusion can be traced to the Budget Speech of Minister of Finance Shri P. Chidambaram.

"The findings of the NSS 59th Round (2003) reveal that out of the total number of cultivator households only 27 per cent receive credit from formal sources and 22 per cent from informal sources. The remaining households, namely, small and marginal farmers, have virtually no access to credit. With a view to bringing more cultivator households within the banking fold, I propose to appoint a Committee on Financial Inclusion. The Committee will be asked to identify the reasons for exclusion, and suggest a plan for designing and delivering credit to every household that seeks credit from lending institutions."[1]

The Reserve Bank of India's (RBI) conception of financial inclusion appears to be even more restrictive. "The Mid-Term Review of October 2005 had urged all banks to make basic banking facilities accessible to vast sections of population with a view to achieving greater financial inclusion."[2] But the measures announced by Governor in April 2006 were in the nature of procedural simplification. For instance, banks should provide a basic 'no-frills' account with nil or very low minimum balances as well as charges, a simplified General Purpose Credit Card (GCC) should be provided without insistence on collateral or purpose and so on. RBI hoped that these measures would go some way towards 'achieving greater financial inclusion'.

The new approach of both the Finance Minister and the RBI to widen the reach of banks or financial institutions in general is a welcome

1. Chidambaram, P. (2006). "Budget Speech", Minister of Finance, Government of India, February 28, p. 11.
2. Reddy, Y.V. (2006). *Annual Policy Statement for the Year 2006-07*, Reserve Bank of India, April 18, p. 56.

departure from the financial sector reforms era of the 1990s. This was an era of exclusion: credit flow to the rural sector shrank, with the banks defaulting on both the credit targets for priority sectors and for agriculture. In fact, there was disenfranchisement of a large number of small farmers, as reflected in the sharp decline in the number of small borrowal accounts of banks during this phase.[3] While this new approach is welcome, it is not enough. To be able to appreciate the fuller challenges of financial inclusion, one has to first understand the phenomenon of inclusive growth, or broad-based decentralised growth, in the real sector.

The Chinese Experience

China, whose macroeconomic parameters are or were comparable to those of India, provides perhaps the most fascinating contemporary example of such inclusive growth. This experience is particularly relevant to India because both have or had an overwhelming proportion of population dependent on agriculture and the incidence of poverty was or is high in both the cases. Today, as Simon Maxwell points out "China's manufacturing power is reshaping the world economy. China already produces between 30 per cent and 50 per cent of World's PCs, DVD players, Cameras and TV sets, 83 per cent of its tractors and accounts for 40 per cent of global cement production. The world capital-labour ratio has nearly halved because of the incorporation of new labour force in the global economy."[4] Analytically, what is important to highlight is that impressive growth in manufacturing—or even the double-digit GDP growth sustained over two decades would not have been able, by themselves, to make a significant dent on the levels of unemployment and poverty.

It was the vibrant rural non-farm sector which played a critical role in the success story of drastically reducing poverty and unemployment. China's Township and Village Enterprises (TVEs) provided increasing job opportunities outside agriculture thereby, augmenting sources of household income.[5] This led to the creation of a whole new economic

---

3. For a detailed discussion, Mujumdar, N.A. (2001). "The New Architecture of the Rural Credit System", Mumbai University, Mumbai; and also Mujumdar, N.A. (2005). "Risk Philosophy", NABARD, Mumbai.

4. Maxwell, Simon (2006). "What's Next in International Development?", *Working Paper 270*, Overseas Development Institute, London, June.

5. Braun, Jochim von, Ashok Gulati and Shenggen Fan (2006). "Agricultural and Economic Development Strategies and the Transformation of China and India", *Annual Report 2004-05*, International Food Policy Research Institute, Washington D.C.

sector which became the most dynamic in the Chinese economy. The rural non-farm sector comprised, "The small-scale food processing plants, machinery repair shops, and increasingly more modern and technologically intensive industries that cropped up to meet growing demand among increasingly well-off farmers and employ millions of people whose labour was no longer needed on farms."

In fact there was a structural change in the Chinese economy. While agriculture accounted for more than 50 per cent of GDP in 1952, its share fell to 14 per cent in 2004. Over the same period, the rural non-farm sector which was practically non-existent in 1952, accounted for one-third of GDP in 2004. As a result of this development, rural poverty which was 33 per cent of the population in 1971, fell sharply to only 3 per cent in 2001.

Indian Basket of Segments

The crux of the whole discussion on inclusive growth in the real sector is that even if the 8 per cent GDP growth targeted in Eleventh Plan is sustained in the coming years, and export growth is maintained at say 15 to 20 per cent, the organised sectors like large and medium industries including service sectors like IT sector, etc. can do precious little to tackle the problems of unemployment, poverty and hunger. In other words, jobs generated autonomously by the normal growth process will fall short of the requirement. The policy thrust will perforce have to be on decentralised, broad-based growth, that is, 'inclusive growth', on which the Eleventh Plan is expected to focus. The financial system, including banks would need to gear itself up to cater to the new segments to facilitate such a growth process. The segments may have been neglected so far and hence banks may not be familiar with their credit requirements, methods of processing, and appraisal of projects relating to these segments. Extending credit support to those segments is in essence what constitutes 'financial inclusion'.

The first step in this direction is to identify the segments of the rural economy which, so far have not attracted much attention by banks or other financial institutions, but which deserve to be focused on in the new strategy. This bunch of segments cannot be called non-farm sector in the strict sense; the important distinction is that banks or lending institutions should look forward to financing sectors or segments beyond crop production. Obviously, the package of such segments cannot be identical with that of Chinese because of different resources endowments, and also priorities. As illustrative of the segments on which banks need to focus, we could identify the following.

Even after the potential of large and medium irrigation projects is fully exploited, about 60 per cent of cultivable land would continue to be under the dry farming system. Hence future agricultural growth will have to be necessarily water-centric. Five interconnected programmes assume significance in this context: (i) watershed development programmes, both micro and macro; watershed development programmes, if properly implemented, have the potentiality of providing livelihood security in the rainfed regions, (ii) renovation of all water bodies linked to agriculture, which have presently fallen into disuse; (iii) correcting the deterioration of public irrigation works, notably state canal systems due to cumulative neglect of repair and maintenance. Poor maintenance has led to loss of water through seepage and hence water use efficiency is very low at around 25 to 40 per cent, as against the 65 per cent norm attainable; (iv) rainwater harvesting and conservation, and (v) equally important is the need to raise water use efficiency, by promoting micro irrigation technology on a large scale through drip and sprinkler irrigation systems.

The second set of segments relates to what can be broadly called diversification of agriculture. This is an inclusive concept which would encompass, animal husbandry, horticulture, dairy development, fisheries and development of wastelands and forests, plantations, soil conservation, drainage and flood control, organic farming with organic seed and compost preparation, food processing, storage, warehousing and marketing. All these impinge directly or indirectly on agricultural development and rural incomes in general. This wide range of activities are illustrative of the segments from which the demand for investment credit and working capital that may emanate and bankers and other rural lending institutions should prepare themselves for meeting these requirements.

Inclusive Growth and Credit Policy

Before we take up for discussion the challenges that financing of segments of the real sector listed above throw to the making of credit policy, three aspects of financial inclusion ought to be spelt out. First, we began with the proposition that financial inclusion is a growth and development imperative. Basically, this is so because broad-based and decentralised growth in the real sector is perhaps the only route to sustainability of high growth and development: Growth imperative because sustainability of say 8 per cent overall GDP growth is contingent upon growth in the segments we have discussed above. Take the case of agriculture. While the Tenth Plan stipulates an average annual growth of 4 per cent, the actual average for the first three years works out to some 2 per cent. Perhaps growth in the irrigated fertile lands like the Punjab-Haryana region has reached a sort of plateau. The thrust for further growth must now come from the rainfed, dry lands. It is in this context, that watershed development, rain harvesting, renovation of water bodies, etc. discussed above, assume significance. Projects relating to these segments offer higher employment in the rural sector where poverty is concentrated and ensure food security to the poor through enlargement of their purchasing power. Inclusive growth in the real sector, thus, ensures growth with equity.

The second aspect relates to viability. The illustrative segments we have chosen to discuss would offer projects which would be viable and therefore bankable. For instance, take any project relating to water-centric development of agriculture. The economic returns on these projects would be such, as to justify the investment on these projects. In addition, there is a consideration that many of these are in the nature of social overhead capital investment. It has become necessary to clarify this point because of the stigma that 'social banking' of the 1960s has acquired in the post-liberalisation era of the 1990s. Take for instance, the recent statement of Shri V. Leeladhar, Deputy Governor, RBI: "Added to these woes, the PSBs were also saddled with some non-viable and loss making branches thanks to the social banking concept thrust upon them by the regulatory authorities in the 1960s."[6] Credit policy designed to persuade banks, to finance the new range of projects must guard against being dubbed as 'social banking'. The projects we have discussed are economically viable and the credit policymakers need not be apologetic about persuading banks or other lending institutions to extend credit support to such projects.

The third aspect relates to the scope of financial inclusion, which has a much wider connotation, than the coverage of all cultivators by institutional credit. The term 'agriculture' should be construed in an extended sense which would, of course, include allied sectors like livestock, fisheries, poultry and forests. Raising rural income levels would involve not only higher agricultural growth but also raising production levels of products like milk, meat, poultry vegetables and fruits. Besides

6. Leeladhar, V. (2005). "Emerging Challenges before the Indian Banks—The Road Ahead", *Reserve Bank of India Bulletin*, June.

promoting diversification of agriculture, there is the need for value addition for increasing rural employment and incomes. Post-harvest activities such as storage, transportation, processing and marketing become important in this context. In addition, investment avenues which go someway towards raising directly or indirectly the production capabilities of agriculture will have to be covered. As the recent Committee on Capital Formation in Agriculture has pointed out the emphasis should be on 'Capital Formation for Agriculture' in contrast to our conventional approach of 'Capital Formation in Agriculture'. "The new strategy for agricultural growth and diversification of agriculture from traditional crop cultivation to horticulture, etc. would require more investment in cold storage, rural road, communication, marketing network and facilities, warehouses, etc. Simultaneously, efforts should be made to revitalise agriculture through introduction of biotechnology and other innovations. This would require substantial increase in investment in research and development for agriculture."[7]

The loan-portfolios of banks and other rural lending institutions, must begin to reflect the more diversified credit support to these emerging areas and not merely support to crop production, important though it will continue to be.

The task of credit policymaker would be indeed arduous. To begin with the composition of the basket of segments we have discussed is so heterogeneous that RBI cannot think in terms of targets for segments or sub-segments. RBI will have to perhaps evolve region-specific baskets and depend upon its persuasive proclivities to induce banks to finance such projects. The focus of policy in the coming years would have to be: first, on sensitising banks about the emerging segments of the economy which need credit support; second, to persuade them to extend credit support to these segments. The task of RBI is difficult because the segments we have discussed are not 'glamorous' like the corporate sector or the export sector. Again, these are segments with which banks are not familiar and hence, initially at least, banks will have to make special efforts to evolve appropriate mechanisms to reach these segments. This brings us to the new architecture of the rural credit delivery system.

Another point which arises in this context is that when micro credit institutions, which we will discuss presently, are involved in the rural credit delivery system, is there a need for instituting some sort of credit

7. Government of India (2003). *Report of the Committee on Capital Formation in Agriculture*, New Delhi, March, p. 21.

guarantee scheme, and/or providing interest rate subsidies? An interesting example is the Chinese experiment of providing micro credit to laid-off workers to enable them to start new businesses. This credit was supported by guarantee scheme and was also subsidised.[8] Whether such incentives, could be provided initially to expand micro-finance institutions in India needs to be explored.

New Architecture of the Credit Delivery System

The new segments of the economy on which lending institutions including banks, need to focus are scattered and dispersed widely. And commercial banks cannot easily access them. Moreover, underlying the present sickness of the rural credit system are two core causes: high transaction costs of such dispersed lending in small amounts, and poor recovery performance. More recent experience has demonstrated that both these problems can be tackled effectively through the instrumentality of micro credit institutions. The experiment of micro finance through the conduit of self-help groups (SHGs) has shown that transaction costs could be reduced drastically and repayment rates can be as high as 90 per cent. Both RBI and NABARD have been spearheading the promotion and linkage of SHGs to the banking system through refinance support and other proactive policies. Three models of credit linkage of SHGs with banks have emerged; SHGs formed and financed by banks; SHGs formed by NGOs but directly financed by banks; SHGs financed by banks using NGOs as financial intermediaries. The second model has emerged as the most popular model. Thus, the programme launched in 1992 has enabled the formal banking system to reach 11.6 million poor households through the conduit of 1.17 lakh SHGs.

The role of micro credit as the most appropriate and economically feasible *modus operandi* in attaining the twin objectives of growth and poverty alleviation is, thus, well established and the rural credit system—commercial banks, cooperatives and RRBs—must move towards spreading this model and spreading this fast. The coverage of poor families today is modest: only 11.6 million poor families out of the total of some 58 million. Secondly, in terms of regional distribution, there is uneven growth of micro-financial institutions. At the end of March 2003, of the total SHGs credit linked with banks, Andhra Pradesh accounted for nearly 40 per cent. Taking four states Andhra Pradesh, Karnataka, Tamil Nadu and

8. Xiaoling, Wu (2004). "Promoting the Extension of Micro Credit", *BIS Review*, 46.

Uttar Pradesh together they accounted for nearly 70 per cent of the SHGs credit-linked and 80 per cent of the total amount of bank loans. There is therefore, the urgent need to replicate this model of reaching rural credit to different segments of the rural sector through the instrumentality of SHGs or NGOs in other states. Of course, NABARD has been playing a catalytic role both in terms of promotional grant support to NGOs and nurturing SHGs. But this is not enough. PSBs, on their part, should also make similar efforts to promote and nurture NGOs and SHGs: because such efforts will be mutually beneficial both to the lending institutions and the beneficiaries of bank credit.

Banking Agents

Yet another model of linking NGOs and SHGs with banks has emerged with the RBI issuing guidelines in February 2006. With the objective of extending savings and loan facilities to underprivileged[9] and unbanked population, RBI has advised banks to use the services of NGOs, SHGs, Micro-Finance Institutions (MFIs) and other Civil Society Organisation (CSOs) as intermediaries in providing financial and banking service. These intermediaries could act as business facilitators or correspondents. Commercial banks do not have to obtain RBI's prior approval for using these intermediaries as facilitators. How far this model would be effective in extending the reach of the banking system, time alone can demonstrate.

Conclusion

It is necessary to appreciate that financial inclusion is a much wider concept than what is implied in the task of bringing all the cultivators into the fold of institutional credit. The latter would continue to be important, no doubt; but that constitutes only part of the story. At this stage of India's development, 'Inclusive Growth' in the real sector has become critical as the Draft Approach Paper to the Eleventh Five Year Plan testifies. The Chinese experience is illuminating in this context. More appropriately, financial inclusion can be regarded as the counterpart of the inclusive growth in the real sector.

Viewed from this broader perspective, the task of credit policy formulation becomes formidable. Financial inclusion becomes a growth and development imperative: Growth, because a high growth in GDP of say 8 per cent per annum envisaged in the Eleventh Plan can be sustained

9. Reserve Bank of India (2006). *Monetary and Credit Information Review*, Mumbai, February.

only if other sectors/segments of the economy spelt out in the article, are activated. Development, because broad-based and decentralised growth is perhaps the only route by which the bulk of the poor can be provided livelihood and food security. The article has identified some of the sectors or segments of the economy which need to be activated with adequate credit support. Many of these sectors are not 'glamorous' sectors like the corporate or export sectors and hence have received little or no support from banks. But the projects relating to development of these sectors are viable and hence eminently bankable.

The task of the Central Bank is thus two-fold. First, to identify such projects which can be activated with the support of bank credit. The projects may be area or regions specific and it behoves the Central Bank to sensitise the concerned banks about these projects. Second, to pursuade banks, particularly PSBs, to increasingly involve themselves in these projects.

Reference to another aspect of credit policy may be made here. In this whole business of promoting larger flow of bank credit to the emerging sectors or segments identified here, is there any need to provide credit guarantee schemes, or interest rate subsidies to specific institutions? This needs to be explored particularly with reference to micro-finance institutions.

Finally, a word about the new architecture of the rural credit delivery system. Obviously, it may not be possible for banks to reach by themselves all the segments we have discussed here. Banks may have to utilise some institutions as intermediaries. We have seen that the SHGs—Bank linkage programme has emerged as the largest micro-finance programme. But SHGs are concentrated in selected states and hence, it has not been possible to replicate this model throughout the country. Recently, RBI has permitted banks to use services of NGOs, CSOs and Micro-Finance Institutions (MFIs) as intermediaries in providing banking and financial services. Depending on the state or region specific situation, policymakers will have to seek ways and means of reaching bank credit to the emerging sectors/segments discussed here. Inclusive growth in the real sectors would seem to depend, to considerable extent, on the success with which the rural credit delivery system extends its support to the process.

Part IV

Development Perspectives

17

CEO Salaries

Don't Bank on Peanut-Monkey Logic

The recent advertisement by the Government for a chief executive officer for the proposed IDBI-converted bank promised 'market-linked compensation' for the CEO and this has raised a furore among public sector banks (PSBs) and financial institutions.

Other PSBs, including the State Bank of India (SBI), are making representations that the pay packets of their top management cadre should also be similarly structured. They want the emoluments of CEOs of PSBs and financial institutions to be broadly in alignment with their peers at ICICI Bank—whose CEO has got market-linked salaries since the institution was delinked from the government.

For instance, while the CMDs of SBI and IDBI get a salary of about Rs. 33,000 a month, the MD of ICICI Bank gets a whopping Rs. 7.8 lakh. While there is certainly a case for upgrading the salaries of these CMDs, it would become necessary to review the basic principle underlying the salary structures of all public sector bodies.

In the process of implementing financial sector reforms, we have unfortunately tried to mimic many American banking practices, irrespective of their relevance to the Indian ethos. Indian reformers quote with glee American management *guru,* James Goldsmith's well-known phrase: "If you pay peanuts, you only get monkeys."

It is time that we debunk this myth. The Enron fiasco demonstrates the depths to which unbridled corporate greed can sink men. Many of the CEOs, who were paid sky-high compensations, led lifestyles akin to the erstwhile maharajas. These princely emoluments, it turned out, produced creatures with rapacious mindsets and more cunning than monkeys. Enron was not an abnormality in an otherwise sound system; the affliction was systemic. In the US, the Sarbanes-Oxley Act and a host of other regulatory measures have been introduced to rein in rogue companies.

Competence, efficiency or a sense of commitment does not vary directly with the size of the salary packet. It would be naive to believe that if CMDs of PSBs were paid salaries comparable to their peers in, say, the Bank of America or Standard Chartered, they would transform them into dynamic institutions generating massive profits.

But some experts, as those in ICICI, seem to believe that financial institutions can be transformed by appointing superstars at a hefty price as brand ambassadors, whatever that may mean. Intellectual servility has been a by-product of the liberalisation process. The approach to reforming the banking system reflects an affinity to mimic the systems of the developed world, especially the US.

India's banking history is a glorious example of total dedication and commitment of professionals. The phenomenal expansion of banking in India in the post-nationalisation period, both in terms of widening and deepening the system, is unprecedented in the history of world banking. Bringing the rural sector, which was practically isolated from the rest of the economy, into mainstream banking was indeed a stupendous achievement.

The travails and tribulations of the officials in this dramatic transformation are chronicled in *Taking Banking to the People*, by Dinker Rao of the National Institute of Bank Management. This should be compulsory reading for all the new entrants in PSBs or financial institutions. It hardly needs mention that the officials at that point of time were not being paid princely sums.

At least those who work in these public sector set-ups should disabuse their minds of this craze for American-scale salaries. Even in the US, the salary of the Federal Reserve chairman is nowhere near that of some of the corporate CEOs.

Recently, a CEO of an MNC in India claimed total emoluments of some Rs. 2 crore a year. In contrast, the RBI Governor earns only around Rs. 6 lakh. Nobody would argue that the responsibilities of the RBI Governor are any less onerous. Nor can it be argued that this wide disparity in emoluments has failed to attract the best of talent to the post of Governor.

This plea for eschewing such sky-high salaries or emoluments should not be construed to mean that there is no case for appropriately raising salaries of professionals in the public sector. The emoluments should be adequate to enable the professionals live in comfort and dignity. But beyond a threshold, the emoluments would fall into the 'obscenely high' category.

There is another myth build up by some management experts that needs to be exploded. That is, if the salaries are low or poor, it would lead to corruption. It should be stressed that corruption is wealth/income neutral. In fact, the Enron scam symbolises the crisis in American capitalism. Most of the CEOs involved were already rich, but that did not satiate their greed for more money or wealth.

Ultimately, it is the work and moral ethos created in the economy and the value system of society that are important. The primacy for eschewing obscenely high emoluments stems from the larger concerns of society. The United Nations Millennium Declaration adopted in September 2000 clearly spells out the task of poverty alleviation:

"We resolve... to halve by the year 2015, the proportion of the world's people whose income is less than one dollar a day and the proportion of people who suffer from hunger.

"We will spare no effort to free our fellow men, women and children from the object and dehumanising conditions of extreme poverty, to which more than a billion of them are currently subjected. We are committed to making the right to development a reality for everyone and to freeing the entire human race from want."

It is in this broader context that the concept of 'shared growth' has become part of the accepted development philosophy.

Only such growth can ensure sustainable development. In other words, if any section or segment of society appropriates a disproportionate share of national wealth, it would be tantamount to depriving other sections of their legitimate share.

As neither the public nor private sectors operate in a social vacuum, the approach to salaries or emoluments should be guided by the larger concerns of society.

Let it be known that dedication, commitment, skills or talent are not contingent upon getting disgustingly high levels of salaries.

18

Delusions of Grandeur

If Karl Marx were alive today to survey the contemporary Indian scene, he would have perhaps exclaimed, "Cricket is the opium of the masses" Halfway through the performance of Satyanarayan Pooja in a temple, the presiding priest pauses and whispers to his assistant, "What is the score?" It is then that I realise that the assistant was watching the India-Pakistan cricket match on the television in the adjoining room and it was his duty to keep the presiding priest informed of the latest score, even when the latter was invoking the blessings of Lord Satyanarayana.[1] I was getting my shoes polished and the *mochi* had an ancient radio blaring forth the commentary on the ongoing India-Pakistan cricket match. "Five wickets down, Saab", the *mochi* dishes out the unsolicited information to me. The Times of India, a highbrow newspaper devotes the entire front page—exclusively to Indian team's victory in the one-day cricket match series against Pakistan. Forget the other news, national and international. So also, the NDTV—a highbrow channel, devotes full 15 minutes of its half-an-hour 9 O'clock news programme to exult in the Indian cricket team's victory.

The return of the cricket heros to India is also being televised by NDTV. A whole new mythology is, thus being woven by the media around cricket. Is it that the print and electronic media, particularly the English media, creates this mass cricket hysteria? Or, is the media merely catering to the demands of the masses? One begins to wonder.

When Amartya Sen won the Nobel Prize in Economics a couple of years back, was there such a mass hysteria? No, cricket is different. It has huge money, the sponsorship, advertisements, cricket players acting as brand ambassadors, and even reportedly, betting. Let there be no mis-understanding. All sports, not only cricket, should be promoted and encouraged because it is one way of improving the quality of life of the people at large. But when, in the name of cricket, students skip classes, officers absent themselves from work, all normal life comes to a standstill, one should begin to think in terms of the impact such hysteria has on GDP or national income. Perhaps the Central Statistical Office (CSO) could make an attempt to assesses the adverse impact that such mass hysteria has on our economic life.

There is a far more disturbing development which the social scientists should sit up and take notice. The hysteria generated by cricket should be seen as part of the larger theme of creating delusions of grandeur around India and ourselves. India is emerging as a super power and as an intellectual capital of the world. Its emergence as a powerful force in the IT sector is, too, well-known to need elucidation. The out-cry in the US against outsourcing by the US Corporates is a testimony to the progress that Indian IT sector has made. Again, take the biotechnology sector. Biocon is already a globally significant enzymes company and it hopes to emerge as one of the top 10 biopharm companies in the world. The world has recognised India's enormous intellectual capabilities. The last few months have seen a number of global pharma majors visiting India for exploring R&D opportunities. As Kiran Mazumdar Shaw of Biocon puts it: "India will certainly be a global R&D hub in the not-too-distant future."

The point is that whether in the field of Cricket, or sectors like IT or biotechnology, India's achievements make the nation proud and these call for celebrations. But the danger that we need to guard against is that the social stupor generated by these grand celebrations should not make us blind to stark realities in other sectors of the economy or segments of the society. In a way these achievements are islands of excellence in an ocean of ordinariness. It is this ordinariness that we need to address immediately with redoubled vigour.

More than a quarter of the country's population, of 260 million people do not have incomes to access a consumption basket which defines the poverty line. More bluntly but, they are in a semi-starvation state. Nearly one-half of all Indian preschoolers suffer from malnutrition. Even when we produce adequate quantities of foodgrains we do not know how to reach them to the poor. Otherwise, how do we explain the fact that India exported about 10 million tonnes of foodgrains in 2003-04. This is at a time when we are not short of foreign exchange. The country's foreign exchange reserves have soared to an embarrassingly high level $110 billion. What is worse, today, policymakers soaked in market theology shun food subsidies for domestic consumption. At the same time, they have no compunction about subsidising foodgrains exports! In some villages in Tamil Nadu students trek 10 kilometers daily to attend school to avail themselves of the free mid-day meal. Take another instance of our concern for the poor and the starving. Under the Food for Works programme, foodgrains are supplied by the Center to States free of cost. But the record of the states lifting of foodgrains allotted for the scheme from the Food Corporation of India (FCI) is disappointing. For instance, against the allocation of 35.33 lakh tonnes, only 21.26 lakh tonnes were lifted in 2001-02. Do the states need to be sensitised about the misery of poverty, unemployment and the state of semi-starvation? Beware of the delusions of grandeur.

19

Investing in Education?

Yes, But What Sort of Education?

Economists have been in search of the alchemy of development since the early 1950s. What is the magic *mantra* by which a developing economy is transformed into a developed economy? In development models it has become axiomatic to postulate that the rate of growth of the economy is determined by the rate of investment. Given the capital-output ratio of a particular economy, it is easy to calculate that X rate of investment will produce Y rate of growth. In this context, investment means fixed investment in terms of investment in plant and machinery, capital equipment and on. It was Professor Theodore Schultz of Chicago University, Nobel Laureate in Economics, who added a new dimension to the concept of investment. He maintained that for a developing economy investment in education of the people is as important, as investment in capital equipment. A given amount of fixed capital investment will be far more productive in an economy with an educated population than that in an economy with uneducated population. This approach has now become part of accepted development doctrine and investment in education is regarded as promoting the formation of 'human capital'. While conceding that education is an essential ingredient in the policy-mix designed for development, the question that needs to be posed is: Investment in education? Yes, but what sort of education? This question has acquired a contemporary connotation because of some recent developments, as I will explain presently. The 32nd Lala Lajpat Rai Memorial Lecture which focuses on the theme 'Human Capital' provides a good opportunity for us to reflect on this important issue.

Let me begin with the citation of three cases. When McCauley introduced English education in India during the British regime, he had never dreamt of developing India. Far from it all that he wanted was to produce an army of clerks to support the steel frame of the British empire.

Second, take the case of Malta, the Mediterranean State which became independent in 1974. Since it had no natural resources, it was advised to develop the tourist industry by providing the necessary facilities for education and training. The then President of Malta is reported to have quipped: "By all means, let us develop the hospitality industry. But let us guard against the country degenerating into a nation of waiters". Third, take the contemporary scenario of Indian IT industry. In spite of the glorious record of growth of the software industry, some thinkers have warned that we should not be complacent with the achievements, lest there is a danger of our ending up as a nation of cyber-coolies, on the analogy of indentured Indian labour of the British empire. Here, the reference is to the proliferation of the so-called 'call centers' which concentrate on 'transcription' jobs. This is certainly not to belittle the contribution of Indian software experts to more sophisticated segments of the industry but only to emphasise that we should move increasingly into the more sophisticated areas. The instances are cited merely to highlight that the content of education is as important as the emphasis on the form of education in general.

This issue has acquired a contemporary relevance with the recent fall from grace of the American capitalist image. Revelations of corporate crookedness and accounting scandals have shaken the very foundations of American Capitalist model. The depth of degradation to which unbridled corporate greed can lead has become all too obvious. The Enron, World com and Xerox, and Global Crossing exposures have unveiled the ugly side of Western style capitalism under which, in the quest for short-term gain, wrongdoings are overlooked. These developments cannot be dismissed, as some apologists of American Capitalism seem to be doing, as isolated incidents. As Professor Lester C. Thurow puts it: "The Enrons and Worldcom are not abnormalities in a basically sound system—scandals are endemic to capitalism". "Furthermore, the A-hold scandal showed, as the Economist put it, that Europe is not immune from America's Corporate ills (*The Economist*, March 1 and 7, 2003). Many other scandals have come to light more recently in France and Italy. In other words, people have lost trust in the measures of corporate performance that they are given and in the people who give them. The Economist sums up the situation: "Chief executives and accountants have become a despised breed, less trusted even than politicians and journalists." (*The Economist*, November 30, 2002). Many of those involved in these scandals were highly educated MBAs or Chartered Accountants, the professions of both of which have now come into disrepute.

In India, we have had our own share of such scams in the stock market, involving Harshad Mehta, the closure of Bank of Karad, and some non-banking finance companies and mutual funds. The collapse of the UTI was the mother of all scams. The more recent failure of the Global Trust Bank (GTB) adds one more instance to the litany of financial misdeeds. The point that we need to underline is that many of the actors involved in these scams were educated men and at least some of them were regarded as financial wizards at that point of time. When we talk of investing in education, is this the kind of education that we have in mind?

What has gone wrong with our education policy? The central point, I am seeking to make is that we should din into the ears of all educated persons whatever be their professional training, be they engineers, scientists, economists, social scientists, administrators, or even humble men and women with elementary education, that our aim is to evolve, not only into an affluent society, but also an affectionate and caring society. We certainly want that India should metamorphise itself into a developed economy from its present state of a poor economy. In the process of so doing, we should not trample upon the basic values of our ancient civilisation.

Accelerating economic growth is undoubtedly a prerequisite for reducing poverty, eliminating illiteracy and disease among the bulk of the population; but this goal is not exclusive of the broader objective of evolving on egalitarian, just, humane and compassionate society. There should, thus, be a synergy between growth and economic and social development.

This brings us back to the basic question: What should be the end-objective of education? Indian philosophy offers a remedy for this sort of 'sickness' in contemporary civilization. It advocates the need to build 'development conscience' among all sections of the population, within a country and across countries. From times immemorial Indian philosophy has maintained that an all-round development of a society is best achieved through the betterment of an individual, which no doubt includes economic well-being but extends well beyond it.[1] Social conscience must be inculcated among individuals, through education at all stages and also professional training. All individuals, must be sensitised, at an young age, to the abject poverty, the squalor, disease and illiteracy that surround us. They must be made to begin to think in terms of what is our *dharma* or

1. Mujumdar, N.A. (2004). "The Development Conscience Factor" in *Economic Reforms Sans Development*, Academic Foundation, New Delhi.

duty towards alleviating some of the infirmities that afflict our fellow human beings. We may begin to think in terms of poverty within a nation and then extend it to poverty across countries. In fact, Indian philosophy regards the earth as one family, *Vasudhaiva Kutumbakam.*

The *Brahadaranyaka Upanishad,* one of the ancient scriptures of India enjoins that our life must be guided by the following three "Da's": "Damyata", that is control yourself; "Datta", that is, give to others; and "Dayadhwam", that is, be compassionate. Thus, we must practice self-control, charity and compassion. Collectively, these three characteristics constitute what has been called as 'development conscience'. Building up such conscience among all sections of population—within a country and across countries—would go a long way towards accelerating economic growth, promoting a 'shared growth' process, improving the quality of life for all stakeholders in the society, and thus, evolving a compassionate society.

The spontaneous response to the recent tsunami disaster provides a glimmer of hope for India. Not only did the private corporate sector demonstrate its sense of social responsibility, but also people from all walks of life—celebrities, professionals, the average householders and even the not-so-well-to-do families, students—rose as one man to wipe the tears of those afflicted by this terrific natural disaster.

It is in such monumental crisis that the core of a society's culture manifests itself. It should be the central objective of all educational institutions—academic, professional or vocational—to inculcate this strong sense of fellow feeling. One does not have to wait for a national calamity to occur for such feeling to express itself: but this feeling should be an integral characteristic of all educated people.

To conclude, let us by all means invest in education but ensure that it is the right kind of education. Unbridled greed, ruthlessness in accumulating personal wealth, insensitivity to surrounding miseries of fellow human beings—these ills characterise the cream of today's educated society. Let us seek to replace this section of society with the new breed of educated people, who would have acquired, as part of their educational equipment, development conscience.

Index

A

B

G

H

I

N

O

P

Q

R

T

U

V

W

Y